Involved in ~~~~

The Life and Message of Vivekananda

MARCUS TOYNE

Involved in Mankind:
The Life and Message of Vivekananda

Ramakrishna Vedanta Centre

First published 1983
© Marcus Toyne

Printed in Great Britain by
Chas. Luff & Co. Ltd., Slough, Berkshire
Cover Design Creative Services Ltd., Hertford

ISBN 0 7025 0040 2

Those who wish to learn in greater detail about the teachings contained in this book are advised to communicate with the Secretary, Ramakrishna Vedanta Centre, Bourne End, Buckinghamshire

For Barbara, with love

Contents

FOREWORD

A good friend, a respected Bishop of the Church of England, recently told me that England had yet to discover Swami Vivekananda.

It is eighty years since Vivekananda passed away. Six years of his most creative period were spent in the West and of these, six months were spent here in England. Some of his profound thoughts were formulated in his meditations here, and as he spoke from the depths of these realisations his words reached into the very souls of those who heard him.

The West, today, is seeking new values and beliefs to sustain itself, and in the life and writings of Vivekananda there is much to stimulate and strengthen this search for stability. The Swami had a deep understanding of both the Eastern and Western cultures, and tried to bring about a synthesis between religion and scientific thought. He interpreted the philosophy of Vedanta to enrich the religious consciousness of the West.

The author of this book, Marcus Toyne, has been stirred by the spirit of Vivekananda. In the pages that follow he has made an effort to study and understand the teachings of the Swami and their relevance to life in the West. The manuscript of *Involved in Mankind* was serialized in the magazine of the Centre, *Vedanta for East and West*. It was much appreciated, hence our decision to publish it in book form.

Swami Bhavyananda

President
The Ramakrishna Vedanta Centre
Bourne End, Buckinghamshire

Preface

"Take the bow of sacred knowledge, lay against it the arrow of devotion, pull the string of concentration, strike the target."

Few men have taken this advice from the *Mundaka Upanishad* to better effect than Vivekananda. I first came across the Swami ten years ago when a friend lent me a tattered book which had been printed and published in the Himalayas in 1907. It was the first volume of *The Complete Works of the Swami Vivekananda* in the Mayavati Memorial Edition. After reading a few pages, I recognised "my" truth, and was lifted out of a trough of annihilating depression into the awareness that, maybe after all, life *was* worth living. Somehow what Vivekananda said, and the way he said it, had an immediate and deep appeal to me; reading his lectures was like eating a good meal after a lifetime of malnutrition. Not only that: the ideas were extraordinarily familiar, and I kept saying to myself, "Of course, that's the way it is, but I'd forgotten. How could I have been so stupid?" This is not to say that I became a Perfect Master in one easy lesson! Alas, the last decade has seen recurrent outbreaks of spiritual amnesia, and Giant Despair has seized the opportunity to immure me in his dungeons for further spells in Doubting Castle. But I've always got out again, and frequently this has been by going back to Vivekananda, who has never ceased to remind me that I am, in reality, a roaring lion, and not a bleating sheep.

There is, of course, no substitute for the eight volumes of *The Complete Works,* and anyone who wishes to deepen his knowledge of Vivekananda, should refer to the bibliography at the back of this book on page 162. My intention has been to create a distillation rather than a digest, and if the result acts as a stimulant, then it will have fulfilled its purpose. Realisation doesn't consist of reading books, it has to be experienced within oneself; but it is still good to find one's intuitions confirmed and strengthened. Vivekananda once said that the first sign of true religion is that a man becomes more cheerful, and one of my guidelines has been to avoid any kind of "heaviness" in the writing of this book. Vivekananda's great gift was to talk lightheartedly about serious subjects, and I hope, in the pages which follow, that the reader will tend to smile rather than frown.

I should like to thank the Ramakrishna Vedanta Centre for all the books that they were kind enough to send me; without those books, I should not have been able to start. If what I have written gives as much pleasure to those who read it as it has done to the one who wrote it, then I shall be delighted. For me, Vivekananda has always been an exciting figure, and his message struck me straightaway as supremely relevant to twentieth century man. That message could be contained in two words, "Be free!" but perhaps that is rather bald advice, taken in isolation. What follows might be said to be an expansion of those two words.

At the time of writing, the world is toppling about us, and the long supremacy of the West is coming to an end. Quite what is to come in the remainder of this century remains to be seen; but one thing is certain, we shall be better fitted to cope with whatever happens, if we have heard and understood the message of Vivekananda. That is why I have taken the liberty of repeating it. If, in some other world, the Swami is in a position to give my effort his *nihil obstat*, then I am content. I have tried to keep to the spirit of the message—here it is.

MARCUS TOYNE

PART ONE:

THE LIFE

Chapter One

ARRIVAL

"Nothing can be evolved which is not already there." (Vivekananda)

Freudians speak of the trauma of birth, and suggest that we spend our adult lives unconsciously yearning to return to the comfort and safety of the womb. Be that as it may, the most extraordinary thing about new-born babies is that they look so impossibly and immensely old. Those wrinkled little faces speak of an ancient time, of ineffable experience, of a forgotten wisdom. In his recent book, *Birth Without Violence*, Frédérick Leboyer put pictures of new-born children alongside photographs of the Buddha, and in both there was that same blissful smile of a contentment beyond words. True, most babies are rapidly galvanized into frenzied and tearful life, and they are not slow to accommodate themselves to a brash new world; the clouds of glory retreat, and the sturdy demands of an emerging ego will no longer be denied. The struggle of life, which must inevitably end in death, has begun.

Parents differ in their attitudes and feelings towards the new arrivals. Sometimes the baby fulfils a long-felt need; often, the birth is taken as a matter of course; occasionally, the child may be seen as a usurper or rival. Saddest of all, are the children who are experienced as no more than a burden or embarrassment, when the parents have seemingly been "careless". In fact, no matter how longed-for or unwanted any baby may be, each birth is intended to happen when it does happen, and to speak of mistakes or accidents is absurd. If we dig our own graves, then assuredly, we also pick our own wombs. However, it is not a choice necessarily in the conscious sense, but a matter of having fitted ourselves for a certain birth in a certain body *by our past actions*. Neither parent nor child should quibble therefore, because both parties can be said to be responsible for the situation.

The baby, then, is thrust into the world, propelled by an accumulation of forces, which explosively insist that he present himself for further duty when the time is ripe. That apparently helpless bundle of bawling humanity may be physically helpless, but he has much to answer for, and he is driven by energies, which will fire him to action, until the allotted fuel runs out, and he is free to go back to where he came from.

That at least, is how Vivekananda saw it, and it is important to be aware of the deeper implications of the idea of destiny, before considering the life of one whose destiny was so outstanding. Of course, we are all men of destiny; we all arrive with a certain force behind us. But it is only in the exceptional person that this force becomes obvious. We can see this when a person is either extraordinarily good or incredibly bad, but it is much less easy to make sense of those who fall somewhere in the middle. Most lives appear to be spent groping in the opacity of darkness, and few feel called upon to find a meaning and a purpose for their existence. This is partially because they haven't got the courage to take leave of their senses, until they are at the point of death; but mainly because they just don't know what is going on. Like billiard balls, they career about the table, sometimes landing in a pocket, sometimes not. There seems to be neither rhyme nor reason about it; everything appears to hinge on flukes and random happenings. It is reserved to the spiritual giants to provide the necessary intensity and brilliance of light, which enables men to see things as they really are, and to appreciate that they are part of an immensely complicated and intricate pattern. Without such illumination, there is the fatal tendency to believe that happiness is attainable in earthly terms. Such a belief is all right in youth, but it begins to lose its appeal as age sets in. In the lovely words of the *Dhammapada,* "Those who in their youth did not live in self-harmony, and who did not gain the true treasures of life, are later like long-legged old herons standing sad by a lake without fish." Gradually the brute facts of transience and decay force their attention on the most doughty of pleasure-seekers, and behind all the gaiety and distraction, a voice quietly but inexorably insists that, in the last resort, all is vanity. It does not require a preacher to make this point: we all know it in our heart of hearts, although we may hide it quite well from other people. Given meaning, the worst of sufferings become acceptable, even welcome; but without meaning, all is chaos and old night. Can there be a more chilling word than "futility"?

Vivekananda came to deliver a message, and, in one way, the details of his life might seem secondary to that message. Yet, in his case, certainly, the medium *was* the message to such a degree, that knowledge of his personal experience is indispensable to a true understanding of his teaching. It was his proud (and entirely justified) boast, that he never taught anything which he had not experienced for himself. That is why what he says rings so true. For all his prodigious memory and startling intelligence, the real power of Vivekananda lay in his utter loyalty to the *facts* of religion; he was never content to be fobbed off with a theory which he had not tested for himself. Nowadays, many people are attracted by exotic stories and esoteric notions of one kind and another: there is a vogue for the spiritually picturesque. For those, however, who insist on the truth, no matter how many cherished fairy tales have to be sacrificed in the process, then Vivekananda is their man. His mission, first and foremost, was to distinguish between the true and the false, and reality must ever elude us until we take this distinction to heart.

Vivekananda was born at 6.49 a.m. on Monday, January 12, 1863 to the Datta family in Calcutta. He was given the name of Narendranath, which means a chief or ruler of men, but his relatives and friends took to calling him Naren for short. The child was born into a land dominated by Western foreigners, mainly the British, but, at the same time, he was heir to the enormous spiritual heritage of the Indian past. His caste was that of the Kshatriyas or warriors, and *The Bhagavad-Gita* tells us that the marks of this caste are an heroic mind, an inner fire, constancy of purpose, resourcefulness, courage in battle, generosity and noble leadership. Naren was to be a Kshatriya *par excellence*.

At the height of his career, Vivekananda was to say that he owed his intellect and his compassion to his father. Viswanath Datta came of wealthy and cultivated stock and achieved considerable success as an attorney-at-law of the High Court of Calcutta. He was very much a man of the world, and could not have been described as particularly religious. However, despite his agnosticism, he never worried about his considerable possessions and therefore had an instinctive understanding of the wisdom of non-attachment. Viswanath had wide interests, being adept in both English and Persian literature, and having a high regard for Islamic culture and the Bible. Naren learnt music at his father's insistence and was to inherit Viswanath's enthusiasm for travel and sophisticated cookery. But probably the most valuable interchange between father and son was at the intellectual level. Naren's native brilliance was channelled into logical and informed argument and the boy grew up to abhor vagueness of expression and to see the need for grasping essentials.

Naren's quickness sometimes led him into rash remarks, as for example when he criticised his father for giving too readily to people whom Naren dismissed as worthless. Viswanath rounded on the precocious moralist and asked him how he could possibly understand the great misery of human life, and told him that when he *realised* it, he would sympathise with "the poor creatures who try to forget their sorrows in the momentary oblivion obtained through intoxicants". It is significant that Viswanath should have used the word "realise" here, a word so beloved of his son in later life.

On another occasion, the boy petulantly asked his father what he had done for him. Instead of losing his temper, Viswanath replied quietly, "Go and look at yourself in the mirror, and then you will know."

Probably the best piece of advice that Naren ever received

from his father was succinct, and redolent of an almost eighteenth century sangfroid, "Never show surprise at anything." In the event, this proved good counsel indeed.

If Viswanath embodied Mind, then Naren's mother, Bhuvaneswari Devi, supplied the perfect counterbalance of Heart, of loving kindness. Vivekananda's lifelong championship of motherhood and the importance of women's contribution to life undoubtedly derived in part from his mother's qualities of love and devotion. Bhuvaneswari's traditional womanly skills ensured that the Datta household was run both efficiently and harmoniously, but she was much more than a mere housewife, having considerable musical ability and a lively appreciation of her Hindu heritage. She could recite large portions of the great Indian epics, *The Ramayana* and *The Mahabharata*, and her son was later to belittle his own phenomenal memory, by saying that his mother had only to read something once in order to have it by heart. The poor and the sick knew that they would always have their needs met by Bhuvaneswari Devi, for whom religion was an intensely practical matter. As we shall see, Vivekananda always emphasised the value of chastity and said that a race must first cultivate a great respect for motherhood, through the sanctification and inviolability of marriage, before it could attain to the ideal of perfect chastity.

Vivekananda himself, however, never married, and in this respect followed in the footsteps of his grandfather who had left home to become a wandering monk. From his earliest boyhood, Naren was attracted to the life of renunciation and longed, with Yeats, "to hear the talk of those naked men". He annoyed his parents by giving food and clothing to passing mendicants, and could never hear enough of his grandfather's experiences: from the very beginning, he knew in his bones that the world could only truly be won by rejecting it, and this despite the fact that he was well aware of his "royal" qualities, which could so easily have been harnessed to worldly ambitions.

Naren was an unusually lively lad, so much so that, on

occasion, his mother found that the only way to calm him down was to douse him with cold water, while chanting the name of Shiva in his ear. This seems to have been an infallible remedy, but as time went by, the boy ploughed more and more of his apparently inexhaustible energy into projects of all kinds. He had a great enthusiasm for pets, and these included at different times, goats, monkeys and peacocks, as well as guinea pigs and pigeons. As for games, he was attracted to any and every sort of sport. When it came to jumping, running, boxing, or any other athletic activity, Naren had no equal. His quick wit, total lack of shyness and endless initiative drew many friends to him, and he early displayed a talent for cooking which was pronounced excellent, "although he was inclined to use too much cayenne pepper"

Other hobbies included model-making on a grand scale (he had a go at creating a miniature gasworks), amateur theatricals and magic lantern shows. He took his friends to see local places of interest and even managed to sneak some of them on board the British man-of-war which had brought the Prince of Wales out to India. A characteristic boyhood story tells of Naren picking flowers from a tree, despite a solemn warning that if he did, a ghost would wring his neck. He waved to his pusillanimous friends below, who had not braved the ghost, and told them how stupid they had been to accept such a ridiculous story, crying, "Don't believe what others say unless you yourselves know it to be true."

Another typical piece of youthful iconoclasm was the time when Naren sampled all the carefully segregated tobacco pipes for visitors to the Datta household. Caste and creed dictated this arrangement, but the boy thought it ludicrous, and said that he couldn't see what difference it made.

The picture which emerges then is of a dare-devil, ebullient boy who would accept nothing on trust, but had to test everything for himself. He was a natural leader and it is significant that his favourite game was that of "King and Court". In this game, the throne was at the top of a flight of stairs leading from a courtyard and no one was allowed to sit on the same level as anyone else. A step was allocated to those who had been appointed Prime Minister, Commander-in-Chief and so on, all being subordinate to His Majesty at the top, who corrected any misdemeanours with a regal frown. Naren had no doubt of his right to the throne, and throughout his career he never lost the royal touch; it was his majestic bearing that impressed everyone at the Parliament of Religions in Chicago in 1893, although there was one person present who observed waspishly that Vivekananda "did not argue that he was a superior person, he admitted it".

However dominant Naren may have been with his boyhood friends, he was never domineering. Sheer force of character made him a leader, but there was another side to him which was ready to submit and adore. This contemplative aspect early declared itself when he bought himself some clay images of the gods, Rama and his wife, Sita, and adorned them with flowers before sitting down in front of them cross-legged in an attitude of meditation. The boy seemed to have an aptitude for meditation which was inborn, and of course he grew up in a country where such an approach was considered quite natural. But what is interesting in Naren's case was that he peremptorily forsook Sita and Rama after hearing one of his father's friends condemning marriage vehemently. Shiva took the place of the now unhallowed couple, Shiva being the third person of the Hindu trinity, the Destroyer, the god of renunciation and the ideal of the yogis.

Naren once asked a schoolmate if he ever saw a light between the eyebrows at night when he went to sleep. The other boy expressed astonishment at this phenomenon, and Naren realized that what he had taken for granted was an experience peculiar to him. He began to pay greater heed to precisely what happened and the sequence was always the same. First, he would see a ball of light, constantly changing colour, which would gradually grow larger and larger, till in the end it exploded and it was as if his whole body was then filled with a white radiance. Later, Ramakrishna was to explain to Naren that such a vision only comes to those who have a great spiritual past.

Another experience which aroused Naren's curiosity was that he kept meeting people and situations, previously unknown to him, that were unaccountably familiar. He rejected the obvious answer of reincarnation and decided that he had somehow had a preview of his present life, and that various scenes and incidents had been shown to him in advance, like "trailers" taken from a film.

Childhood's end for Naren was marked by a mystical experience which occurred in 1877 when the Dattas were travelling to Raipur in the Central Provinces. The boy lay in a bullock cart and, in the rather fulsome words of his Eastern and Western disciples, "was charmed with the exquisite grace and beauty with which the Almighty Creator had adorned the rugged bosom of the earth". But then he saw a large beehive in a cleft between some huge rocks: his senses swam, and he was so overpowered by the sheer miracle of the living world, that he lost consciousness (or, to be more accurate, moved into a different level of consciousness). Swami Nikhilananda tells us in his biography of Vivekananda, that "even after returning to the sense-perceived world, he radiated joy".

In reading of such an experience, one either knows what is meant, or one is left quite cold, because it does not correspond to anything meaningful. There is no way of expressing this kind of ecstasy in words, and in the pages which follow this problem is going to arise again and again. The Sanskrit term *samadhi* was described by Yeats as "a final state of complete wakefulness . . . where the soul, purified of all that is not itself, comes into possession of its own timelessness". It is doubtful that Naren plunged straight into this "final state" as he gazed entranced at the beehive, but he certainly crossed the frontier from that perception which we call ordinary, into a country where reality is less diluted in intensity. Mystics are people who are vouchsafed glimpses into the heart of things, when for a moment they realize that what they took to be the natural order, was not what it seemed. For Naren, the sight of that busy commonwealth of bees somehow triggered off what he had always known, but had temporarily forgotten; as a result, he lost touch with his boyhood self in the bullock cart, and made contact with that universality of consciousness which was to be the overriding concern of his life. However, in the years of adolescence which were to come, the lesson of the beehive faded as Naren began to put his formidable mind through its paces. Vivekananda could never have spoken to the West so effectively if he had not been through the intellectual mill.

Chapter Two

INTELLECTUAL DIAGRAMS

"I developed concentration without the power of detaching my mind at will; and the most intense suffering of my life has been due to this."
(Vivekananda)

It is very much the fashion these days to stress the dangers and limitations of being "intellectual", especially when it comes to trying to make contact with God. The aim, we are told, must be to rise above mental processes, and attain to higher levels of apprehension; otherwise, there is a strong possibility of finding that our supposed holiness is no more than a bundle of notions which bears little relation to what we say or do. Such spirituality tends to be fanatical and unrealistic, because it is disconnected from the heart.

No one knew better than Vivekananda that mental symbols in the mind can be just as idolatrous as more concrete religious imagery. Intellectuals are particularly at risk in this respect, because they are able to make their idols so plausible and respectable, not realizing that they have allowed their minds to become their masters. Nevertheless, a *controlled* mind is of incomparable value in the search for truth; indeed, anyone of high mental ability who tries to bypass reason is guaranteed to make a fool of himself. In 1895, when Vivekananda was in London, he said to an interviewer from the *Westminster Gazette*, that whatever in his teaching might appeal "to the highest intelligence and be accepted by thinking men", the adoption of that would be his reward. There could be no question of negating reason, but rather of fulfilling it.

When Vivekananda came to the West, he saw the need for showing his hearers the weaknesses of their own arguments *in their own terms*. Like all good teachers, he took his pupils from where they were, and that is why he was so slow to mention the name of Ramakrishna; he knew that this would initially be a stumbling block for the Western mind. He saw that in order to build a new structure of ideas, he had first to shatter intellectual conceit through reasoning, scientific argument and philosophy; then, and only then, could he move on to his own ground. As he remarked to a disciple, once Westerners found themselves off their moorings "through their utmost intellectual reasoning", they would be sufficiently humble to listen "in a real spirit of truth". Vivekananda had to be the highly educated and sophisticated person that he was in order to get a hearing, otherwise he would have been dismissed as no more than a quaint Oriental—had that been the case, we should never have heard of him. Nothing impresses a man more than to hear a foreigner speak his own language, and speak it superlatively well. The English-speaking peoples, in particular, are terribly arrogant when it comes to other languages; they see no need to learn them, because in most parts of the world English is understood. What shook the vast audience at the Parliament of Religions was that a "native", complete with turban, should not only make himself understood, but that he should do so with such consummate brilliance.

Naren first heard a few English words at his mother's knee, but he did not take to the language straightaway. After all, this was the barbarous tongue of India's uncouth Anglo-Saxon overlords, and as such could not commend itself to a family as fiercely proud as the Dattas. It is perhaps difficult for us to appreciate just how uncivilized the English seemed to cultivated Indians. Besides there was the humiliation of being governed by these savages! Naren first went to school at the age of six, but was rapidly removed because he was picking up vulgar words from the other children which upset his parents' susceptibilities. A private tutor was hired, and Naren quickly began to show his exceptional intelligence and outstanding memory. At seven, he knew most of a Sanskrit grammar by heart, and could recite large portions of the *Ramayana* and the *Mahabharata*.

In 1871, when the boy was eight, he went to a school where his reluctance to learn English was overcome, and he proved to have an unusual flair for the language. We have already seen that Naren was very lively, and at school he rarely sat down if he could help it, but was forever moving about the room to wherever his curiosity drew him. One of the teachers got so irritated by Naren one day, who had got a fit of the giggles, that he seized him by the ears and lifted him up on to a bench! One of the ears was badly torn in this incident and no doubt Naren's faith in his teachers was rudely shaken. Characteristically he came back to school the next day refusing to be frightened by what had happened.

In order to understand the kind of education which Naren received from his adolescence onwards, one must never forget that India was ruled by the British, and that the British took the view that it was their God-given task to provide the benighted natives with the kind of education they deemed proper. Sir Charles Wood's educational dispatch of 1854 had stated that "we are desirous of extending far more widely the means of acquiring general European knowledge". To be fair, most Indians had received very little in the way of education in the past, and whatever may have motivated the English, the changes which came were highly beneficial and paved the way for later independence. Education was given a tremendous stimulus by the rule that government offices should go to those who had a good knowledge of English, and by 1867 the first three universities had been founded in India at Calcutta, Bombay and Madras. These universities were modelled on the London examining model, though not with the same standards as London. Despite all the old gibes about babus boasting proudly of having failed their B.A.'s three or more times, some Indians made excellent use of the new opportunities. Of course there were elements of absurdity and tragedy in imposing an alien culture on India (vide E. M. Forster's *A Passage to India*), but as far as Vivekananda was concerned, it enabled him to fulfil his destiny as a world teacher. He wrote later in a letter that the British Empire with all its drawbacks was "the greatest machine that ever existed for the dissemination of ideas". Certainly he took full advantage of the "machine".

Between 1877 and 1879, while the Datta family was in the Central Provinces, Naren's formal education suffered, so that when he got back to Calcutta, he had to master three years' lessons in one year. He passed the exam at the end of the year with flying colours, and his father gave him a watch for doing so creditably. Meanwhile he was reading widely in English and Bengali and adopted the rather risky technique of leaving things till the last minute, when it came to exams. Unlike lesser mortals, he got away with it by cramming in whatever was required at astonishing speed. Four books of geometry, for example, were mastered in twenty-four hours, and he mopped up Green's massive *History of the English People* in a record three days. Naren's secret lay in his intense concentration, and his knack of speed-reading which enabled him to take in the contents of a page at a glance. Quite often he would stay up all night reading solidly, keeping himself awake with strong cups of tea and coffee.

The truth is that Naren was, as he said himself, born for the life of a scholar. Nothing gave him greater pleasure than to be at his books, his superb mind effortlessly absorbing whatever he placed in front of it. His favourite subject was history, but he also read a good deal of philosophy and familiarized himself with the ideas of Aristotle and August Comte, Schopenhauer and Kant. He was particularly attracted by John Stuart Mill and Herbert Spencer, and was later to quote from them in his celebrated lectures.

But Naren paid a high price for this concentration, because he did not discover how to detach his mind at will once the task at hand was completed. Thus he built up mighty mental muscles which gave him terrible cramps and spasms as he wrestled with one new idea after another. Being basically a very honest person, he was constitutionally incapable of believing anything merely because it suited him. Consequently, as

Christopher Isherwood has graphically put it, "His doubt was his passion."

He had at this time a Johnsonian appetite for argument, and like the Great Cham, brandished a rapier of ready and caustic wit. He would accept nothing through fear or outside pressure, and the stern young agnostic submitted himself to such austerities as sleeping on bare boards with only one blanket. Yet he was no puritan, but loved parties and was always a welcome guest with his songs and general good humour.

It is difficult to speak of purity without arousing either disbelief or mockery, but the fact remains that Naren was determined at all costs to avoid getting embroiled in sexual adventures. This was dictated neither by primness nor repression; he knew instinctively that to give way to passion in his particular case would have been disastrous. Despite pressure from parents, relatives and friends, he rejected marriage and asked angrily if they were all trying to drown him. "Once married," he insisted, "it will be all over with me." As in the case of any other young man, Naren's body demanded fulfilment, and rebelled when this was not forthcoming. He resorted to drastic methods to curb his lust and once, to cure a fit of passion, sat on a tub of burning charcoal, and on several occasions refused to succumb to the charms of women who set out to seduce him. In due course, Ramakrishna explained that this self-control had by no means been in vain; if a man can be celibate for twelve years (and this means in mind as well as in body), then "he can understand and grasp very subtle things which would otherwise elude his intellect."

Naren, however, had yet to meet his Master, and although he was working so hard, and apparently going from strength to strength, he was consumed with a tremendous dissatisfaction. He did not *know* what life was all about, and worse, he could find no one else who seemed to know either. Intellectual diagrams were all very well, but they did not slake his thirst for truth. Cleverness had declared itself bankrupt.

Early in the nineteenth century, a group known as the *Brahmo*

Samaj had been founded by Rammohan Roy; this was a response by Indian intellectuals to the Western challenge. Members of the *Brahmo Samaj* protested against the polytheism of Hinduism, they disapproved of the worship of images and saw no need for gurus in the search for meaning in life. At the social level, they were violently opposed to caste distinctions, demanded greater equality for women and wanted more education for the masses. Before all else, the *Brahmo Samaj* gave pride of place to reason, and it is hardly surprising that such a movement should have attracted Naren. Here perhaps, he felt, lay the answers to his uncertainties and conflicts. But the trouble with the *Brahmo Samaj* was that it had no roots in its own culture, and as the French revolutionaries had discovered, the goddess of Reason is no substitute for the living God. Argument and debate were all very well in their way, but somehow one grew out of them, and besides, they did not seem to lead anywhere. What Naren desperately wanted was *reliable* knowledge—he had had enough of hypotheses and theories. He went on looking into all sorts of subjects (he studied Western medicine to find out more about the brain and the spinal cord, for example) but his real appetite was for a unifying factor, for the One behind the many. "Sir", he asked again and again, "Sir, have *you* seen God?" The sages looked embarrassed, and one of them paid him the compliment of saying that he had a true yogi's eyes, but none could give him a positive answer. Surely there must be someone who had had *direct* experience of reality—or was it only something that one read about in books? Just as one never seems to meet anyone who has actually seen a real dead ghost, so Naren never seemed to encounter first-hand information.

The Principal of the General Assembly's Institution which Naren attended to read for his degree, was a Scot named W. W. Hastie. It was Professor Hastie who discerned true genius in Naren and prophesied that he was bound to make his mark in life, and, in a curious way, he was instrumental in his pupil's making that mark. One day the professor was giving a lecture about Wordsworth (one of Naren's favourite poets), and the poem under discussion was *The Excursion*. Hastie began to consider the whole phenomenon of exalted states of consciousness—that state of being when a man seems to enter another dimension of experience. He paused in his discourse, and added that he had only known one person who "had realised that blessed state, and he is Ramakrishna of Dakshineswar".

The other push in the direction of Dakshineswar came from a cousin who saw that Naren was in earnest about not wanting to marry, but wishing to follow another path. "All right then," said the cousin, "if you seriously want to live a spiritual life, you ought to talk to Ramakrishna. You won't find anything at the *Brahmo Samaj*."

And then in November 1881, Naren was invited to a friend's house to entertain the guests with his singing and playing. He stood before them, full of vigour and vitality, his incomparable eyes sweeping the assembly, and his songs were mellow and haunting with a power which moved the audience to an appreciation which was more than applause. One of the members of that audience was particularly moved, so much so that he made enquiries about the young man, and sought an introduction with him. The upshot was that Naren was invited to visit his admirer at Dakshineswar. He accepted, by no means convinced that a meeting with this rather simple-looking old man would lead to anything particularly valuable. Could such a person have met God? On the face of it, it did not seem very likely, but it was worth a try. As is the way with the great turning points of one's life, Naren went on his way blissfully unaware of what lay in store for him. Perhaps it was just as well.

Chapter Three

THE BLACK GODDESS

". . . I happened to get an old man to teach me, and he was very peculiar."
(Vivekananda)

In point of fact, Ramakrishna was not all that old when Naren first met him: he was only in his mid-forties. People, of course, age much more rapidly in the East, but quite apart from that, for Naren, Ramakrishna epitomised the Wise Old Man in the Jungian archetypal sense. Nevertheless, at first, Ramakrishna's simplicity and total lack of artifice did not strike Naren as marks of wisdom, and it was to be several years before he could accept the "Old Man" as his Master. We can be glad that this was so, because gradual conviction carries much more weight than overnight conversion. Naren's scepticism stemmed from great intellectual integrity, and in order to be true to himself, he had to test and test again before he would believe. It has been well said that Vivekananda, as the world knew him, was the spiritual power, Ramakrishna, in another form. What was implicit in the Master was made explicit by the disciple. Western historians find it hard to credit that a recluse from the world is of much earthly use: withdrawal is seen as abdication from responsibility. What they fail to see in Ramakrishna's case, is that his chief disciple turned out to be one of the best communicators in modern times. The true teacher, as Vivekananda insisted, is one who can throw his whole force into the tendency of the taught, and this was exactly what Ramakrishna did with his star pupil; he gave everything he had learnt to a mere boy, in whom nobody else had much faith, with the absolute knowledge that the results of this transmission would be world-shattering.

What Ramakrishna needed was a "voice", someone sufficiently energetic, gifted and dedicated to put across ideas which had never died, but had been awaiting resuscitation for thousands of years, until such time as human beings were sufficiently developed to receive them. Ramakrishna, as a virtually illiterate Bengali, was in no position to hold a dialogue with the doyens of his age; just as Jesus required a Paul, the sage of Dakshineswar relied on a Vivekananda to spread the good news outside India.

Ramakrishna started life as plain Gadadhar in a remote Bengal village. His father's horoscope stated that Gadadhar would eventually live in a temple surrounded by disciples, that he would found a new institution for teaching religion, and be revered for generations to come. A remarkable prognostication! However, the lad had to grow up first, and he was soon a great favourite in the village with his lively and fearless approach to life, his sense of fun and his talent as a mimic.

Gadadhar was only seven when his father died and thereafter the boy received a smattering of schooling in Calcutta, enough to convince him that education seemed to be geared entirely to material ends. Unlike Naren, Gadadhar found little to detain him in books, but became dominated by the desire to get truth direct, rather than filtered, diluted and distorted through other men's minds. He had already had a foretaste of reality in a classic Zen experience as a boy, when he saw some white cranes flying against a black cloud, and this moved him so deeply that he went into Samadhi.

Having rejected education, Gadadhar started his spiritual practices at the temple of Dakshineswar on the banks of the Ganges a few miles from Calcutta. Priestcraft was considered most improper for a true Brahmin because priests in India were regarded as people who made a profit out of religion by charging fees for their intermediary services. The temple in which Gadadhar officiated, contained an image of the goddess Kali. For many, the name of Kali will be associated with the ritual stranglings of the Thugees; it is difficult for Westerners to

31

understand how the cult of Kali can be anything but abominable, and trebly difficult to see what such worship can have to do with the one true God. It is perplexing to find that Vivekananda could, at one and the same time, be devoted to Kali, and yet also be committed to the Advaita proposition that All is One. Western logic blenches at the apparent clash here.

The black basalt image of Kali at Dakshineswar is quite small, less than three feet in height, and the goddess stands on the prone body of a white marble Shiva, who lives on a thousand-petalled lotus. Kali is festively dressed in red silk adorned with jewelled ornaments, while round her waist is a girdle of severed arms and her neck is encircled with a grisly necklace of skulls. She has four arms, and sticks out her tongue in the most unladylike way.

So far, so bad—at least to the sensibilities of one accustomed to Christian iconography. But worse is to come. In one of her left hands she holds a decapitated head, while the other brandishes a bloody sword! The right hands, however, are less horribly engaged: one confers blessings, while the other is raised in a gesture which signifies, "Be without fear!"

Kali represents the Divine Mother, the Primal Energy; she embodies in herself creation and destruction, love and terror, life and death. Nikhilananda clarifies her role when he writes that "to the wicked who have transgressed her laws, She is the embodiment of terror, and to the virtuous, the benign Mother". Beauty or the Beast lie therefore entirely in the eye of the beholder.

If one thinks dispassionately of the crucifix, it depicts a man dying in agony on a cross. Tradition enshrines this as the Saviour suffering to save our sins, but to the uninitiated, it could quite reasonably be taken to reflect a sado-masochistic preoccupation with the morbid. So let us not be too quick to take exception to blood-boltered Kali, who is both wicked queen and Blissful Mother, blissful because she leads her devotees through the Valley of the Shadow of Death, and enables them to overcome the fear which trembles within them.

In December 1970, Franz Stangl, former commandant of the Nazi extermination camp at Treblinka in Poland, was interviewed in Düsseldorf Prison. Stangl, together with others, was responsible for the deaths of some 400,000 people during the war. After the German defeat, he was sentenced to life-imprisonment as a war-criminal, so that by the time he was interviewed, he had been in gaol for a quarter of a century—time which he had spent reflecting on the enormity and horror of what had happened at Treblinka. Somehow his imprisonment had purged him of the evil of the past, and he was no longer the same man. Amongst the questions put to him was this one:

"Was God in Treblinka?"

"Yes," replied Stangl, "yes, otherwise how could it have happened?"

The Shadow is as much a part of the divine economy as the Light, and if we look at Kali aright, we shall see that she strikes a true balance between the destructive forces on the left hand, and the creative energies on the right, which bid us be of good courage. She is telling us no more than the truth about life, the inescapable fact that living on this planet never ceases to be a challenge. It is by meeting and overcoming resistance, that we come to self-knowledge; without that incessant tension, there would be no growth. That is why lotus-eaters of one kind and another are such depressing people—they have ceased to fight the good fight, and as a result, have succumbed to the paralysis of inertia.

All this should be borne in mind, when considering the young priest at his devotions at Dakshineswar. Gadadhar had no wish to be anaesthetised by the narcotic properties of ritual; hour after hour, day after day, he stared at the image in front of him, and wondered what lay *behind* the black goddess. Indeed, he became so absorbed with this conundrum, that the details of temple ritual went by the board; bells failed to ring, and candles flickered out. Eventually he got so desperate to see the living

Kali, that he seized the sword which hung in the temple and was just about to cut his throat, when his world was unmade. He had staked his life on revelation, and Kali at last relented by admitting him to her mysteries. The whole insubstantial pageant of the everyday world disintegrated and vanished into thin air, "and left not a rack behind". All that Gadadhar could see was "an .infinite shoreless sea of light; a sea that was consciousness". He looked far out into this limitless ocean and saw "shining waves, one after another, coming towards me". He was overwhelmed by the waves and sank down into unknown depths where he panted and struggled and finally blacked out. When he regained normal consciousness, his first words were, "Mother, Mother!", and after that extraordinary experience, he could never again be as other men are.

The other temple officials thought that he had gone off his head, so that he was banished by them from his beloved Kali and took refuge in a nearby wood. In the period which followed, he sat, oblivious of time and space, in a state of total abstraction. Vivekananda tells us that "he could not tell when the sun rose or set, or how he lived". He would certainly have died of starvation if his relatives had not placed food in his mouth which he swallowed mechanically. After a while, he was taken home where he became a little more outwardly "normal", and it was felt by his family that marriage would bring him fully to his senses. So Gadadhar, aged 23, "married" a little girl of five. This was not quite as bizarre as it sounds, because in India such unions were really little more than betrothals at first. In the following year, Gadadhar went back to Dakshineswar and completely forgot about the existence of his bride. When, thirteen years later, she sought her husband out, she saw immediately that her task must be to serve him and learn from him, rather than bear his children and take him back to the world. Gadadhar never consummated the marriage, but remained resolutely continent throughout his life. Fortunately, his wife, unlike her Western sisters, did not see in this, grounds for a divorce.

In the period at Dakshineswar before the arrival of his disciples, Ramakrishna (as we shall now call him) underwent a series of spiritual disciplines, and in the course of these, reached the insights which made him a Master. The keynote of these insights was renunciation: Ramakrishna eliminated one thing after another in his single-minded zeal for God-realization. He vowed never to touch money in any shape or form; he rejected sex, as we have seen, and aimed to see the Divine Mother in all women instead of an object of lust; he refused to criticise or condemn others. Teachers came to tell him of the different Indian sects and to initiate him into Yoga and other practices. Ramakrishna was determined to know the truth about *all* religions, and to this end, he lived for a time with a Moslem holy man, at another period sat at the feet of a Christian saint, and even brought himself to cut his beloved Kali in two with the sword of knowledge in order to reach an understanding of non-dualistic Vedanta. He conquered the whole idea of being distinctively male, by living with a group of women, and dressing, thinking and behaving like one of them throughout his stay. Humility was won by secretly visiting a pariah's house and cleaning out the latrine. In the course of these disciplines, at one point he reached an ultimate realisation of total unity with God for six months, but was recalled to earthly life when the Mother told him that he must defer the luxury of eternal bliss until he had accomplished the work he had to do.

Gradually Ramakrishna enunciated the principles which his chief disciple was to amplify to such good effect; first, one must form character; secondly, spirituality has to be *earned*; and thirdly, a man is then in a position to give what he has realised to the world. "Then," said Ramakrishna, "when the lotus opens, the bees come of their own accord to seek the honey; so let the lotus of your character be full-blown and the result will follow."

He contended that many paths could safely be followed to reach the goal of realisation. For some it might be appropriate to identify with the Self, and say with Christ, "Before Abraham was, I AM." Others' might feel drawn to the way of devotion which rejoices in the fact that "Thou art, O Lord, and all is Thine." Probably most would find the path of "Thou and I" most attractive, in which the servant seeks to serve his Master, or the son loves his Father in Heaven. "In the perfection of any of these three ways," said Ramakrishna, "a man will find God."

And so he climbed from rung to rung of the ladder of perfection, starting as a priest, and moving through successive phases of devotion, asceticism, sanctity and, ultimately, realisation. Some regard Ramakrishna as the Avatar or God Man of the age; Vivekananda himself wrote in a letter to one of his brother Swamis, that he had not the least doubt that his Master was God Incarnate, but he added the important rider that people must be allowed to find out for themselves, "you cannot thrust these things upon them".

After one of his London lectures, Vivekananda was approached by a distinguished personage with white hair who said he had thoroughly enjoyed the lecture, but nevertheless, he felt that he had been told nothing new. The Swami replied, with some vehemence, that he had never tried to be original in his teaching, but had only one aim and ambition in life—to tell the Truth. On his last visit to America in 1900, Vivekananda underlined the extent of his debt to Ramakrishna when he said that if there had ever been a word of truth, a word of spirituality, that he had spoken anywhere in the world, he owed it to his Master, and only the mistakes were his.

This chapter does no more than give the bare bones of Ramakrishna's life prior to Naren's arrival at Dakshineswar. My purpose has been to create an impression at least of Ramakrishna, before embarking on the extraordinary story of Naren's first meetings with his Master and his subsequent training.

Chapter Four

MAN-MAKING

"The readiness is all." (Hamlet)

Everyone, consciously or unconsciously, is striving for freedom, but each seeks for a freedom within his understanding. Some hope to be emancipated by having plenty of money, others imagine that sexual fulfilment is the answer, while the intellectually gifted believe that release will come by accumulating and digesting a vast store of knowledge. It takes a very long time, and a good deal of suffering, before it dawns on the seeker that such solutions are, at best, provisional. They all turn out to be false summits on the way up the mountain, and no sooner has one peak been reached, than another higher one appears in the distance. Naren saw this in his late teens, and understood that the futility of laying up treasures on earth is more than a form of words. He enjoyed a fine physique, a first-class mind, and highly refined emotions, and yet none of these gifts satisfied him. Although he never entirely gave up hope, he teetered on the edge of the badlands of atheism, and his only refuge was the ineradicable knowledge that he thirsted for a truth which he intuitively sensed lay beyond the finite world. It was this thirst that drove him to Dakshineswar. For him, God was as vital for survival as a precious gulp of air to a drowning man. The old aphorism held good that until the pupil was ready, the teacher would not arrive. As Vivekananda was to put it, "You may thrust your head into all the four corners of the world . . . you will not find religion anywhere until your heart is ready for receiving it and your teacher has come." In other words, unless the craving in the heart is absolutely genuine, then nothing happens. The pilgrim must, besides, be pure (Vivekananda said that the text, "Blessed are the pure in heart" is all we need to know) and enormously persevering.

Before a teacher can be accepted as a true guru, the pupil has to be sure that he has met with one who has knowledge of the spirit, who is without sin, and who has no ulterior selfish motive, but is driven purely by love.

A teacher, in short, is a *sine qua non* in the spiritual life; for the spirit to be quickened, the impulse must come from another soul. When the crucial meeting takes place between teacher and taught, it is as if a star has risen on the horizon of consciousness, and as the training proceeds, another bigger star comes, and then a still bigger one, until at last the sun itself rises, and all the lesser lights are eclipsed. In that admirable book, *The Flame and the Light*, Hugh I'Anson Fausset explains that "the aim of the Master is to prove himself superfluous, since what he essentially is, the disciple is". For this to happen, the disciple has to make an unconditional surrender; without such total submission, spiritual illumination can never come. This surrender is the very reverse of self-abasement in the Uriah Heep style, but there can be no question of submitting to a Master until there is complete faith and trust in him. The ego may be an encumbrance, but we cannot guard it too carefully and jealously, until we are absolutely sure we are giving it away to the right person; otherwise we may find ourselves possessed, rather than released. The tragedy of totalitarianism is that it demands the individual, but denies the Self; God, on the other hand, demands all, and gives everything in return.

The first thing which Ramakrishna noticed about Naren at their initial meeting at Dakshineswar, was that here was a young man who cared very little about his personal appearance. This was due less to sloveliness, than to a complete lack of concern about the external world. His eyes were turned inward continually. Naren, however, was sufficiently extrovert that day to sing a song, and after this Ramakrishna drew him to one side, away from the others who were present, and suddenly burst into tears. Much to Naren's dismay, he found himself being addressed as Nara, an incarnation of Narayana or Vishnu, and in the midst of his raving and weeping,

Ramakrishna managed to blurt out, "You have come back to take away the sufferings and sorrows of mankind."

Naren left as soon as he decently could, deeply disturbed by the encounter. His first thought was that Ramakrishna must be "a monomaniac", and yet, at the same time, he "could not help acknowledging the magnitude of his renunciation". But what had really shaken him to his foundations, was the old man's answer to his question, "Sir, have you seen God?" The reply had been immediate and unequivocal, "Yes, I have seen God, I see Him as I see you here, only more clearly . . . if one cries sincerely for God, one can surely see Him."

Why should a man who had seen God conduct himself so oddly? Was it seemly to get so emotional with a complete stranger at the very first meeting? Surely it was unreasonable to behave like that—the man *must* be mad. And yet, and yet, . . . there was a quality about him which suggested that he really *did* know God. Before his hasty departure from Dakshineswar, Naren promised that he would make a further visit.

In the event, Naren did not get to Dakshineswar until a month later, and this time, he made his way there on foot. If the first meeting had been unsettling, the second was infinitely more so. Soon after his arrival, Ramakrishna placed his right foot on Naren's body, and the effect was literally shattering. ". . . first of all I began to see that the houses—rooms, doors, windows, verandahs—the trees, the sun, the moon,—all were flying off,—shattering to pieces as it were—reduced into atoms and molecules . . .". After that prelude, the next stage involved the complete destruction of the consciousness of being a separate self; it seemed that "the entire universe was about to vanish into a vast, all-devouring void". Naren thought he was dying and cried out in panic, "What are you doing to me? I have my parents, brothers, and sisters at home!" At this, Ramakrishna laughed and touched Naren's chest with his hand, at which the world returned little by little, and Naren again "began to see the houses, doors, windows, verandahs and other things". More reassuring still, he came to himself.

Years later, a disciple was to ask Vivekananda if this extraordinary experience could be attributed to "a derangement of the brain", to which the Swami witheringly replied, "Do you take me, at last, to be a crack-brained man?" However, at the time, Naren himself wondered if he had indeed suffered "a derangement of the brain". Had he been hypnotised? Given his considerable willpower, why hadn't he been able to resist the old man's influence? What had come over him? All his assumptions had been undermined and his mind paced up and down inside the cage of his conditioning, shaking its leonine head in fretful perplexity. Typically, once Naren had recovered from the first blow to his self-esteem, he was determined to fathom the mystery, come what may.

Within a week, he was back at Dakshineswar again for a further session with the lunatic who seemed so perturbingly sane. He approached Ramakrishna warily, ready to defend himself in case he was again taken by surprise. But with a touch, the young man fell into a swoon, and while he was unconscious, Ramakrishna asked Naren who he really was, what his task in the present incarnation was to be, and when he would die. In the absence of his controlling and limiting ego, Naren was able to answer these questions from the standpoint of his superconscious Self, and Ramakrishna learnt that the boy had attained perfection even before his birth, that he was "a great soul, perfect in meditation", and that, when the time came, he would immediately relinquish the physical body with a strong effort of will.

On another occasion, Ramakrishna had a vision in which he saw seven sages whose forms glowed with preternatural brilliance. A child of light approached one of the sages, rousing him from his contemplation and said, "I am going down there and you must come with me." The sage nodded his assent, and then returned to his beatific vision; after that, part of him detached itself and descended to earth in the form of a bright light. Ramakrishna explained to his disciples that the sage was Naren, and he was the little child: they had been companions from the beginning of time.

What is one to make of such visions and experiences? One does not wish to be lured into a world of fantasy, and it is significant that Vivekananda said again and again that he was interested only in reality. Neither he nor Ramakrishna were practitioners of the mythopoeic art, and they were nothing if not honest men. One is driven to the conclusion that they were doing no more than describing facts as they experienced them.

Once Ramakrishna was fully satisfied that Naren was the right man for the job, he set about training him so that eventually a complete transference of powers could be made from Master to disciple. Ramakrishna said that there are eighteen manifestations of power which can be found in a human being; two or three of these are enough to win a man name and fame. Naren had all eighteen! The Master's chief fear was that his protégé might well abuse his powers, and he was therefore concerned as much to restrain as to encourage the young man.

Fortunately, Naren had more appetite for truth than power, and was not prepared to take anything on trust. Although he could see the complete sincerity of Ramakrishna's affection for him, he suspected that this very affection could be a source of delusion. "You are fond of me," he told his Master, "and you want to believe that I'm a great man—that may be why you have these visions." Ramakrishna smiled indulgently, secure in the knowledge that he was no mere water-snake, but a deadly cobra whose bite was fatal. Naren, for all his sturdy resistance, was bound to surrender in the end.

For six years, Naren saw Ramakrishna twice a week, and unlike the Master's other disciples, he was told repeatedly that *his* path was entirely different from theirs. He could eat what he liked, smoke to his heart's content, and contradict Ramakrishna as the spirit moved him. Many thought him arrogant and pig-headed, but the Master saw through to the real person, the Vivekananda in the making; other devotees might be like pots and pitchers, but Naren, for Ramakrishna, was "a huge water-barrel". At the same time, the old man was annoyed when his favourite took it upon himself to tell the others what he thought was good for them. When, for example, Naren criticised another disciple for his image worship, Ramakrishna accused him of spiritual bullying and reminded him that it is enough to have faith in one aspect of God, "but never get it into your head that your faith alone is true and that every other is false". For most people, the formless aspect of God cannot be realized either easily or quickly, and faith must find its first focus in that which can be perceived. "Know for certain," said the Master, "that God without form is real and that God with form is also real."

For spiritual power to be safely and successfully transmitted, the donor must step down the current to the right voltage for the recipient, otherwise damage can be done. Naren earned a stern rebuke from Ramakrishna for forcing the pace of a fellow-disciple's growth, by touching him and throwing him abruptly into a deep meditation for which he was not ready. It was explained to Naren that he had not only interfered with the other man's evolution, but he was also frittering away his own power before he had accumulated enough.

And so the training continued, always with the emphasis on the idea that energy must be conserved, and the only way to achieve this is by constant restraint. True strength, as Vivekananda said again and again in his lectures, lies not in giving way to impulses and desires, but in refusing to give them their head; otherwise, like unruly horses, they will pull us to destruction. Desires, just as much as horses, must be properly broken, before they can be safely harnessed.

Meanwhile, Naren's educated contemporaries were appalled to see their friend caught in the meshes of what one of them described as "an uncouth, supernatural mysticism". Naren, for his part, cared less and less for the opinion of the world, and determined to gain reliable knowledge which would be beyond debate or discussion. Just before taking his finals, he felt an utter revulsion for academic study, but nevertheless, he persevered to obtain a good degree. Soon after that, he was put to the test more severely than ever before in his life.

In 1884, his father died, leaving many debts and having
made no provision for his family. Overnight the Dattas were
paupers and the whole burden of responsibility fell on Naren.
With brutal speed, the young man discovered that when it
comes to survival, there is no place for the weak. He refused to
go under, but did all he could to make enough money in various
odd jobs to keep the family going. Ramakrishna heard rumours
that his best-loved disciple had rejected religion as useless, and
was finding solace in wine and women. Afterwards, Naren
admitted that he had been close to atheism, and that he had
been "exceedingly cross with God", but there was no truth in
the allegations of debauchery. More than one woman tried to
seduce Naren by offering him money, but he rejected such
propositions with the robust recommendation that they should
"give up these filthy desires and remember God".

This period of temptation in the wilderness culminated in
nervous and physical collapse, when quite suddenly the clouds
cleared away, and he realized that he was "absolutely
indifferent to the praise or blame of the world . . . secretly, I was
preparing to renounce the world, as my grandfather had done".
At this critical moment, Ramakrishna appeared and took
Naren back with him to Dakshineswar.

After this, the training was intensified still further, and
Ramakrishna decided that the time had come for Naren's
understanding of Kali worship to be made complete. The
young man tended to be rather disdainful of the use of images as
we have seen, but one day, to his astonishment and joy, he saw
that Kali was more than a black goddess—She appeared to him
as the Divine Mother, and She was actually alive. Ramakrishna
told his disciple that he could ask Kali for anything he wished,
and before entering the temple, it seemed obvious to Naren that
the sensible thing to pray for would be material help so that he
could support his family. However, no sooner was he in the
Mother's presence, than all such prudent considerations fled,
and he said,

"Mother,—grant me discrimination, grant me detachment,

43

grant me divine knowledge and devotion, grant me that I may see you without obstruction always!"

Ramakrishna was, of course delighted by this and assured Naren that his family would always be adequately provided for (which proved indeed to be the case).

Towards the end of 1885, cancer of the throat was diagnosed in Ramakrishna and it was evident that his life was coming to an end. He made it clear that the other boys who had been drawn to Dakshineswar, should be in Naren's charge, and by January of the following year, there were in fact twelve disciples, who were to form the core of the future Ramakrishna Order.

Meanwhile Naren was told in season and out of season of the absolute necessity for renunciation. "One must renounce!" reiterated the dying man, pointing to his crossed legs, "if one thing is placed upon another, you must take away the one to get at the other. How can you get at the second thing without removing the first?"

No doubt because Naren had so fully integrated this idea, he was ripe for a state of consciousness in which all differentiation disappeared: a state in which oneness ceased to be a notion, and became a living reality. Ramakrishna knew well enough that for Naren to become a great teacher, it was essential for him to know just what the highest kind of *samadhi* amounted to. At the same time, he could not be permitted to remain in that exalted condition: he had to be "damped down" to some extent, because there was work for him to do. Once the work was accomplished, then the treasure box would be unlocked again, and he would know everything, just as he had when he was in Samadhi—but not before.

In the final handover, Ramakrishna gave Naren everything that he had and was left "as poor as a beggar". Bereft and forlorn, he wept at the enormity of the loss, but all was as it should be; the training was over, and the old man had successfully transferred his powers to someone who was to shake the world out of its long lethargy with an unprecedented display of intellectual and spiritual brilliance. The Master was now free to leave his pathetically emaciated body and murmur, like that earlier Avatar, "It is finished."

Ramakrishna did not die until he had gone through considerable suffering, but throughout it all he remained amazingly cheerful,—more so in fact than his disciples. For them, the fact that their Master was about to leave them filled them with dismay; Naren alone did not gave way to despair, but did all he could to keep the others in good heart. At last, the end came, and Sri Ramakrishna gave up the body. He had promised that before he went, he would cast his whole secret to the winds, and now the secret was entrusted to his chief disciple. He had left the boys in Naren's care with the instruction that they should practise their meditation and worship, and that they should not go home. The Master had made his last will and testament, and it was now up to the beneficiaries to do justice to the legacy. Of all the disciples, Naren was given the lion's share, which was fitting for a person of such majestic stature; his task now was to translate what he had learnt into action. With Ramakrishna's departure, Vivekananda had arrived.

Chapter Five

WALKABOUT

"With few wishes and few cares, and leaving all sins behind, let a man travel alone, like a great elephant alone in the forest." (The Dhammapada)

Naren did not adopt the name of Vivekananada until he left for America in 1893. However, we shall refer to him from now on by the name which took him to fame, and ignore the various pseudonyms he assumed at different times in his period of wandering. At the same time, the mantle of Vivekananda never totally eclipsed Naren; the Swami's smile remained boyish to the end.

The importance of the years between Ramakrishna's death in 1886 and the decision by Vivekananda to go to the United States, cannot be overestimated. At first, he was filled with a wanderlust and restlessness, which drove him from one end of India to the other. Even as late as 1892, a friend noted that "he looked like one who had a tryst with destiny and was not quite sure when or where or how he was to keep that tryst". He had given up everything—status, security and possessions—and as a sannyasin, or itinerant monk, he belonged to no religion, but was committed to a single-minded search for realisation beyond theories, beliefs or dogmas. As Vivekananda himself defined it, the sannyasin "makes complete renunciation of all worldly position, property and name, and wanders forth into the world to live a life of self-sacrifice, persistently to seek spiritual knowledge, striving to excel in love and compassion and to acquire lasting insight". By 1893, he could remark that such a great power had grown within him that sometimes he felt that his whole body would burst. If ever a man was fully primed for action, that man was Vivekananda.

But this is to anticipate: we must return to that August day in

1886 when the crestfallen disciples mournfully returned from the cremation of their beloved Master. In the face of death, it was difficult indeed to remember Ramakrishna's eternal verities, and there can be little doubt that, had it not been for the encouragement and enthusiasm of Vivekananda, the Ramakrishna Order would never have come into existence. Not that the young disciples were offered anything in the way of comfort or consolation in the conventional sense; renunciation was the order of the day, and the boys were told that the more circumstances were against them, the more manifest their inner power would become. Parents and relatives of the renunciates were annoyed and baffled by the apparent waste of talent at the house which had been rented at Baranagore. Here, as it seemed to them, was a group of able-bodied and intelligent young men who, in their zeal for rejecting the way of the world, were behaving in a thoroughly immature and irresponsible manner. Vivekananda, however, held firm to his promise to his Master that, come what may, the boys should not return home. Instead they lived at Baranagore and submitted themselves to intense discipline, extraordinary austerity and the leadership of a man who had only one thought—freedom.

So great was the disciples' devotion to Opus Dei, that the tedious business of eating was frequently neglected as they applied themselves to an endless round of prayer and meditation. It was not uncommon for periods of meditation to start at three in the morning and go on without a break till four or five in the afternoon. The food, when it *was* served, was of the simplest, and the monks between them possessed only one decent set of clothes which was used by whoever had to go out and look respectable.

Vivekananda had no wish to see his charges sinking into intellectual torpor, and he fed their minds with a rich diet of Western and Eastern philosophy, Indian epic literature and an in-depth analysis of the various kinds of yoga. Like all good teachers, Vivekananda knew when to relax the pressure, and there were frequent sessions of music and singing to keep up the

47

boys' morale. The disciples were much given to laughter because their teacher had no sympathy with a gloomy approach to religion; indeed, he laid it down as an axiom that the infallible mark of a truly religious person is that he is cheerful, whatever happens.

One night, as the boys sat in meditation by the fire in the garden, Vivekananda told them the story of the great renunciation of Jesus, and the disciples all solemnly pledged themselves to renounce the world. Some of them, prior to that night, had perhaps been a little uncertain about whether they were fully committed to the monastic life; they had in some sense been serving a novitiate. But after the night of the Dhuni fire, they were dedicated men, and it came as no surprise when they discovered that their decision had inadvertently been made on Christmas Eve.

As Vivekananda was fond of saying, with a smile, it takes a little hard work to become spiritual, and he was aware that his work with the boys at Baranagore must not be allowed to curtail his duty to himself. He had to make what D. H. Lawrence once called "the great resolution of aloneness and singleness of being", that great resolution after which it is possible to take the next purposive step into the future. It seems to be the peculiarity of the truly great that they have to be alone from time to time; they withdraw from their fellows in order to be able to serve mankind at large. To this end, Vivekananda set out on his travels from the monastery, initially for a few days or weeks, but later for much longer periods. For the purposes of this chapter, we shall treat the wandering period as being of a piece, although in reality it was considerably fragmented.

In his travels throughout the length and breadth of India, Vivekananda absorbed a phenomenal amount of information about his mother country. For the first time, it really came home to him that his people were dying of hunger and suffering from every other kind of deprivation. What had previously been mere head-knowledge, became a reality which aroused his intense concern and compassion; his desire for personal realisation now took second place to the desperate needs of his fellowmen. A brother-disciple has admirably summed up the significance of this time:

"He was constantly on the lookout for new experiences . . . constantly gathering ideas, making contrasts and comparisons, saturating his mind with the religious and social ideas of every province, studying various systems of theology and philosophy and finding out the inherent worth of all the varied Indian peoples whose life he closely observed."

He travelled light, exceedingly light: a begging bowl, pocket copies of *The Gita* and *The Imitation of Christ* (he had a tremendous and abiding admiration for Thomas à Kempis), a few scraps of clothing, and a staff. He accepted a present of a beautifully carved rosewood pipe from a Maharaja, but usually refused all gifts. As a sannyasin, he strove to be quite unattached to the few things he did own, always giving away any possessions which aroused admiration. A prized hookah, for example, went to a cook; while he gave his precious staff, which accompanied him on all his wanderings, to a young American who took a fancy to it.

For food, he relied entirely on what he was given, and on one occasion made a vow that he would eat only what was offered him without asking. He was just at the point of collapse, when a man literally chased him with food and insisted on his eating it.

Of course, this way of life took its toll on Vivekananda's health, and this goes a long way towards explaining the physical sufferings of his latter days. He was not prepared to make any concessions to the demands of the body, coming close to death as a consequence more than once. As with St. Francis, so for Vivekananda, the body was Brother Ass, and had therefore to serve its master, however much it might protest.

It was really from July, 1890 onwards, that Vivekananda set off on his own in earnest, and his farewell remark to Ramakrishna's widow (known after her husband's death as "the Mother") was that if he could become a man in the true sense of the word, then he would return, but otherwise, never!

49

In the course of the following three years he met people at every level of society from maharajas to the lowest of the low. He was later criticised for his association with the great men in the land, but his rejoinder was that the only people who had the power to alter India, were her Princes and their Dewans. Throughout his travels, he never forgot that his prime objective was somehow to alleviate the lot of the common people. He realised that to offer religion to men who were starving was little better than an insult; before all else, they needed food and shelter, education and medicine. It was hard and bitter agony for him to see with his own eyes the terrible poverty of the masses and as he said to Turiyananda in great emotion, "My heart has grown much, much larger, and I have learnt to feel. Believe me, I feel it very sadly."

The main reason for his going to America was to raise money for the salvation of the poor in India, and so great was his sympathy with the downtrodden and the humble, that he learnt something of what it meant to bear the sufferings of the whole world. Nikhilananda sums the whole matter up, when he writes in his biography that Vivekananda "came to know how he could make himself a channel of the Divine Spirit in the service of mankind".

Some of the more distinguished and learned men who met Vivekananda during this period, were mystified as to why a person of such outstanding gifts should choose to live the life of a vagrant. The Maharaja of Alwar, for example, asked how it could be that a great scholar, who could easily have earned a handsome sum of money every month, should go about begging. Vivekananda looked him straight in the eye and said, "Maharaj, tell me why you spend your time constantly in the company of Westerners and go on shooting excursions and neglect your duties to the State." To his great credit, the Maharaja took this calmly and replied, "I cannot say why, but no doubt because I like to." "Well," said Vivekananda, "for that very same reason do I wander about as a fakir."

Another interchange with the Maharaja of Khetri deserves

mention and comes across best in the Boswellian manner:

MAHARAJA: Swamiji, what is life?

VIVEKANANDA: Life is the unfoldment and development of a being under circumstances tending to press it down.

Many who met this unusual sannyasin, marvelled at his easy command of English and Sanskrit, his intellectual force and encyclopaedic knowledge. There is the delightful story of the time he was travelling by train and shared a compartment with a couple of Englishmen. With typical arrogance, these two servants of the Raj, assumed that the "native" could not understand them, and they therefore spoke both offensively and coarsely about Indians in general, and about their fellow-passenger in particular. Vivekananda kept his counsel, but when the train stopped, he leant out of the window and asked the station-master for a glass of water in fluent, idiomatic English. The white men, in an ecstasy of embarrassment, apologised for their earlier rudeness and expressed surprise at Vivekananda's complete lack of resentment. "My friends," said the Swami imperturbably, "this is not the first time that I have seen fools!" Flushed with anger, the Englishmen moved forward menacingly, but did not make a fight of it, partially because they were impressed by their companion's powerful physique, but even more by the look in his eye.

I also like the tale of the superintendent of police who inveigled Vivekananda into his house and then suddenly accused him of being the ringleader of a conspiracy. The Swami looked at his accuser, who was a man of mean proportions and meagre build and made a remark which put the superintendent in his place. "If I had been a criminal and conspirator, there would be nothing to prevent me from wringing your neck before you could call out for help. As it is, I leave you in peace." Needless to say, he left unmolested.

Time and again, it is the *spirit* of the man that impresses one during this time. He thought nothing of telling a Dewan who had taken exception to image worship, to spit on his master's photograph, and when the man demurred, he thundered, "You

51

refuse to spit on it because you see in this photo the shadow of the Maharaja's form ... thus it is with the devotees who worship stone and metal images of gods and goddesses."

Yet there were times when his courage nearly forsook him, and he came close to despair. He knew he had actually seen and talked with the ideal man, and yet he did not seem able to match that ideal; his life was apparently muddled away in vain and he experienced moments of utter helplessness. At one stage he even had second thoughts about being a sannyasin, but then he found himself face to face with a tiger. This proved to be a beneficent shock because, with a sudden surge of energy, he remembered his true identity, "I am He!"—whereupon the tiger turned away, and slunk back into the jungle.

One of Vivekananda's most vehement assertions as a teacher was that we should never judge others. Even the most wicked person may have good qualities that we entirely lack. "The woman in the street, or the thief in the gaol, is the Christ that is being sacrificed that you may be a good man. Such is the law of balance—both sides of the shield must be seen." Vivekananda himself learnt this lesson on the eve of his departure for the United States. The Maharaja of Khetri had invited his beloved sannyasin to come to a party. Vivekananda stood in an outer courtyard and heard the voice of a girl singing, and felt that, as a renunciate, it would not be right for him to associate with a woman of that sort. The girl heard of this, and was filled with sadness at the rejection.

"O Lord," she sang, "look not upon my evil qualities!
Thy Name, O Lord, Is Same-Sightedness."
Outside, the Swami heard these words, and stood rebuked: filled with the realisation that all men (and women) are truly equal in the eyes of God, he swept aside his earlier over-nice scruples, and came to the party after all.

These and many other experiences combined in their cumulative effect to convince Vivekananda that he must cross the seas and bring the message of Vedanta to the West. A critical moment was reached at Cape Comorin, the southernmost tip of India, when he swam out to a rock, careless of the sharks which infest those waters, and "the great resolution of aloneness and singleness of being" at last bore fruit. With greater clarity than ever before, he understood that India must be revived by the twin ideals of renunciation and service: the seed was sown of an organisation dedicated to helping others, particularly at times of crisis such as famine or pestilence. In order to finance such an undertaking, he had to go to the countries who held the purse-strings.

News had reached India that an unprecedented gathering was to take place in Chicago—a Parliament of Religions. It seemed obvious to those who had met Vivekananda that he was the ideal person to represent Hinduism at this Parliament. There was no shortage of sponsors, the Maharaja of Khetri being particularly keen on the venture. Vivekananda had very mixed feelings: he was not sure of himself as a public speaker, he yearned to remain obscure, and above all, he was not yet choicelessly aware that this was the right course of action. But at last he had a vision, in which he saw the figure of Ramakrishna walking from the seashore and beckoning him to follow. All uncertainty vanished, and he knew that the die was irrevocably cast.

He was given the name of Vivekananda by his friend, the Maharaja of Khetri, and Vivekananda means, "he who is blessed with spiritual discrimination". No name could have been more apt. When finally, he set sail for the United States on May 31, 1893, he looked like a prince in a silken robe and turban he had been given. The other passengers on the *Peninsular* might well wonder at this magnificent figure standing by the ship's rail, but the Swami, for all his cheerfulness of demeanour, knew that he had embarked on more than a sea voyage. He was on his way to the young and lusty land of America where men cherished the very things which he had been at such pains to reject—gold, reputation and pleasure. As the ship drew away from the quay, he nodded, amused and appalled at what lay ahead, and said under his breath, "Verily, from the Land of Renunciation I go to the Land of Enjoyment."

Chapter Six

BIRTH OF A NOTION

"When I meet really religious people, we are friends at once, no matter what name we give to the divine Will that made us and moves us."
(Lavinia in *Androcles and the Lion*)

Just before he left India, Vivekananda made a startling remark to Turiyananda, which on anyone else's lips would have savoured of megalomania. "The Parliament of Religions is being organised for this (pointing to himself). My mind tells me so. You will see it verified at no distant date." It is only now, ninety years on, that the full force of this prophetic remark can be appreciated. Of all the delegates who attended that great gathering in 1893, only one name still lives, and that name is Vivekananda. The joke is that the Parliament was convened in the belief that the Christian faith was at long last to supplant all other religions; after this, it would be self-evident (even to those groping "in a dimmer illumination") that Christianity contained all the truth there was in pagan beliefs "and much more besides, revealing a redeeming God". Thus spake the Rev. Dr. John Henry Barrows, Pastor of the First Presbyterian Church of Chicago, Chairman of the General Committee, and responsible for carrying out the elaborate preparations for the Parliament. Dr. Barrows was not alone in this: others deplored the very idea of a Parliament of Religions, because they saw it as "treason against Christ", while the Archbishop of Canterbury refused to attend, on the grounds that it would not be right for Christian delegates to discuss religion on equal terms with the representatives of other faiths. All men might be equal, but assuredly, Christians were more equal than others.

The Hindu delegate, meanwhile, took full advantage of his first sea voyage, to investigate everything he encountered en route. He delighted in the Buddha in Colombo; at Canton, he visited a Chinese monastery; in both China and Japan, he was thrilled to discover Sanskrit manuscripts written in old Bengali characters. It took him time to get used to life on board ship, especially keeping track of his possessions, and he was still very much the innocent abroad by the time the *Peninsular* docked at Vancouver. He travelled on to Chicago by train and arrived there in mid-July, only to find to his dismay that the Parliament had been put off till September. He had hardly any money and, as he later confessed to his friend, Professor Wright, initially in America he was almost out of his depth and even feared he would have to give up his accustomed way of being guided, and learn to cater for himself. He soon rejected this "horrid piece of mischief and ingratitude", and made the most of being in Chicago by visiting the World's Fair, which was being held there as part of the great Columbian Exposition. He was greatly impressed by the inventions he saw, the more so because this kind of technological know-how was exactly what India so sorely needed. His enjoyment of the Exposition was marred by the fact that his "pagan" appearance attracted so much ribald interest; he determined to get himself some Western clothes which, apart from being less conspicuous, would also serve to keep him warm! Vivekananda's sense of being a stranger in a strange land was accentuated by learning that he should have come to the Parliament as the representative of a recognised organisation. His countrymen had sent him off with the best will in the world, but had completely neglected to make any proper arrangements, believing that their beloved Swamiji would automatically be *persona grata* in the United States. He was told curtly by the American authorities that it was too late for him to be registered as a delegate. As his resources had almost run out, he took a train to Boston, which he had gathered was a less expensive place to live. On the way, he providentially met a Miss Kate Sanborn who invited him to stay at her house, *Breezy Meadows* in Metcalf, Massachusetts. He was then introduced to J. H. Wright, Professor of Greek at Harvard University, who immediately saw a quality in

Vivekananda which made him determined that this remarkable Indian should attend the Parliament. As he said humorously, "To ask you, Swami, for your credentials, is like asking the sun to state its right to shine!" Everything was fixed up, including a ticket to Chicago, but even then Vivekananda's adventures were not over. He managed to get lost in the northeast part of Chicago, which was inhabited by German-speaking citizens who couldn't understand a word he said. Nothing daunted, he spent the night in a huge empty wagon in the railroad freightyards. On waking the next morning, he was extremely thirsty and "smelling fresh water", he made for Lake Shore Drive, an exclusive residential area. His attempts at begging for food from door to door met with incredulous rebuffs, until he lighted on the house of the Hale family. Mrs. Hale guessed he was a delegate and, after giving him a substantial breakfast, personally escorted him to the Parliament and presented him to Dr. Barrows: Vivekananda's faith in being led through all his difficulties had been vindicated and as he wrote a little later to Professor Wright, he now clearly saw "that He who was guiding me on the snow tops of the Himalayas and the burning plains of India is here to help me and guide me".

The Parliament of Religions was an undertaking, the like of which had never been seen before: for the first time, representatives of the world's great religions were to meet and have the chance freely to expound their beliefs to a large Western audience. Admittedly, the whole enterprise could never have got off the ground, had it not been for Christian evangelical support: and yet ironically enough, despite this bias, in the long run, the Parliament proved more destructive than otherwise to narrow sectarianism.

At 10 a.m. on Monday, September 11, 1893, the Parliament opened at the Art Institute of Chicago in the Great Hall of Columbus. In the colourful language of one of Vivekananda's eastern admirers, this was "a Parliament not filled from the hustings and polling booths, but from the temples and pagodas, the synagogues and churches and mosques of the world". The delegates filed into the hall and mounted the platform, led by Cardinal Gibbons, splendidly arrayed in the scarlet cloak of his office, and the audience of seven thousand rose to its feet. A great organ pealed out with some thunderous introductory bars, and the congregation sang the hymn, "Praise God from Whom all blessings flow" at the tops of their voices. As the echoes of that mighty anthem died away, the Cardinal, seated in the centre of the platform on his iron throne, solemnly led the congregation in a recital of the Lord's Prayer, filling the Hall of Columbus with an immense murmuration. The chief chronicler of the Parliament was afterwards breathlessly to exclaim that "the supreme moment of the nineteenth century was reached".

It was not only Cardinal Gibbons who made a splash of colour on the platform; he had to contend with serious sartorial competition from his fellow-delegates, not least from the member for India, who was "clad in gorgeous red apparel and wore a large yellow turban". But the artifice of dress alone would not have been enough to make Vivekananda so outstanding in that august assembly: his handsome face glowed with an inner fire and the audience had marked him out as a person of consequence before he opened his mouth.

Vivekananda did not actually speak until the afternoon of that first day; he was asked to do so earlier, but declined because he was paralysed with nerves. His heart was fluttering and his tongue nearly dried up in the face of such a massive scrutiny. As it turned out, this attack of stage fright was all to the good, because by the time the Swami had plucked up the courage to make his address, the audience was much in need of a change of atmosphere, having been submitted to very formal speeches so far. Vivekenanda had no notes prepared, and when he stood up to speak, his opening greeting came across with a spiritual force which mere words on a page cannot hope to convey. "Sisters and Brothers of America . . ." After that he could not go on; the audience broke out into two solid minutes of wild cheering and clapping. It was an extraordinary tribute to the sheer presence of the man; intuitively, the message had reached those listening thousands that here was one who spoke with authority, for he was a man of realisation. If the other delegates had spoken for themselves and their sects, Vivekananda spoke for God—and that was what made all the difference.

Once the uproar had subsided, the speaker went on to make a plea for toleration stating that "we believe not only in universal toleration, but we accept all religions as true". Equipped with a superb baritone voice, Vivekananda was able to make himself heard at the very back of the hall (this, of course, being long before the days of microphones). Emma Calvé, the celebrated singer of the time, suggested that his voice had "the vibrations of a Chinese gong", while someone else was put in mind of a 'cello. Suffice it to say, that Vivekananda in that opening speech at the Parliament of Religions, established an immediate reputation as an orator of unusual brilliance, and thereafter, could never shake off the doubtful privilege of being a celebrity. Few men have become famous less cheerfully; after all the ovation he had received, the Swami returned to the privacy of his hotel room and wept bitterly for the loss of his anonymity, fearing what the American publicity machine would do for him, now that he was a name to conjure with.

Yet, if there was sadness, there was also joy, joy that he had caught the American ear so successfully. Now, at last, he could unleash the power which he had husbanded so carefully over the years and give his eternal message to the people of the West, so skilled in matters of business or technology, and yet so ignorant, when it came to the things of the spirit.

The American press was quick to observe that success was not turning Vivekananda's head. The *Boston Evening Transcript* noted that the Swami had merely to cross the platform to be applauded, but that he accepted this "in a childlike spirit of gratification, without a trace of conceit". On the other hand, one Reeves Calkins, showed a more dog-in-the-manger attitude, when he wrote that he "did not greatly admire the magnificent ease with which Vivekananda waved aside

Christian history and announced a New Star in the East". In point of fact, the Swami knew more of Christian history than most Christians, and there could be no question of his announcing a New Star in the East—his task was, in his own words, to pour old wine into new bottles, and he never aspired to any kind of novelty. It was enough to tell the old, old story in such a way as to catch the interest and imagination of the modern ear.

The Parliament of Religions lasted for seventeen days and during that time, more than a thousand papers were read. Every day, the sessions began at 10 a.m. and continued right through the day till 10 p.m. The organisers soon realised that it was a good policy to keep Vivekananda till near the end of the day, when the audience was flagging. After half an hour or more with the Swami, they revived wonderfully, as they were told to love God for God's sake, to strive for purity, and to attain to that universal individuality which can only be reached by abandoning "this miserable little prison-individuality". He insisted that man is not travelling from error to truth, but from truth to truth, and that unity in diversity is the plan of nature. In the address he gave at the final session on September 27, he summed the whole matter up by saying that "each must assimilate the spirit of the others and yet preserve his individuality and grow according to his own law of growth". It was ridiculous, he said, to think in terms of the exclusive survival of one religion and the destruction of all the rest; rather should we help and not fight, assimilate and not destroy, seek harmony and peace and not foster dissension. As he had pointed out in an earlier talk on *Why We Disagree*, anyone who believes that his religion is the one and only true religion, is like a frog in a well who thinks that his well is all that there is to be known.

Typical of the response to this was that of a Jewish intellectual, who remarked long afterwards that, after hearing Vivekananda, he realised for the first time that his own religion of Judaism was true. It was not a question of changing one's faith, but of each man coming to see the essential truth of his own particular approach to the divine.

Vivekananda emerged from the Parliament as its greatest figure, and several newspaper columnists expressed the view that it was, to say the least, lacking in tact to send missionaries to a land so deeply imbued with a living spiritual tradition. Lucy Monroe put this trenchantly enough in her contribution to *Critic* when she wrote that "the impertinence of sending half-educated theological students to instruct the wise and erudite Orientals was never brought home to an English-speaking audience more forcibly".

Granted that few Orientals could compare with Vivekananda in wisdom and erudition, Miss Monroe nevertheless had a valid point to make here. And it is a melancholy fact that there were many at and after the Parliament of Religions who clung to the notion that the only right attitude to take towards religions other than Christianity must be one of "universal, absolute, eternal, unappeasable hostility".

Fortunately, there were those for whom Vivekananda's message of universal tolerance and a common basis for all religions, not only made sense, but admirably expressed what they had often entertained as a possibility, but had never been able to put into words. It is true that Emerson and others had paved the way towards a "transcendental" religion, but it was left to Vivekananda to give this idea a practical application for people of widely divergent opinions and temperaments.

The Swami had made no plans as to how long he would stay in America once the Parliament had finished. He had already more than justified the faith of the Maharaja of Khetri and others who had sent him across the seas, but the work had only just begun. He was determined to earn money to finance the schemes for India and the Indians which were so dear to his heart. To this end, like so many before and since, he set out on a Grand Tour of lecturing which was eventually to take him all over the United States. In the course of this tour, his original

61

aim of making money for his fellow-countrymen became modified as his eyes were opened to the spiritual poverty of the American people. We shall end this chapter with a few words of Shankara, which explain why Vivekananda gave himself so unstintingly to his Western audiences.

"There are pure souls, calm and magnanimous, who do good to the world spontaneously as does the spring, and who, having themselves crossed the dreadful ocean of life, help others also to cross it, without any motive whatsoever."

Vivekananda was such a pure soul, and Shankara's description is particularly appropriate to the last nine years of the Swami's life.

Chapter Seven

THE AMAZING MR. KANANDA

"It is better to wear out than rust out." (Vivekananda)

American newspapers of the 1890s did not worry too much about getting names right; one marvels at the variants on the words, Swami Vivekananda, which appeared in print. "S. V. Kyonda" suggested an African origin, but it would be hard to guess where "Mr. Sivanei Yiveksnanda" hailed from. Many articles saluted "the dusky gentleman" as a Raja, whilst others described him as "the high priest from India", or "the Buddhist monk". Some even turned him into a Reverend; my favourite is "Rev. Swarri"! The lecture bureau, which hired the Swami, felt that "Kananda" looked well on their advance posters, and in the early days, Vivekananda was presented in the guise of a travelling entertainer in the vaudeville tradition.

For Americans, the East was "mysterious" and they had little desire to dissipate the fascinating air of mystery. They doted on tales of Indian mothers who threw their babies to crocodiles; of fakirs lying on beds of nails; and, of course, it was well known, that little boys regularly vanished into thin air as the grand finale of the Indian Rope Trick. All this was absurd enough, but far worse was the complacent assumption that the white man's Christian duty lay in forcibly imposing his beliefs onto the benighted "heathen". Vivekananda used sometimes to amuse his friends by singing all the verses of the famous missionary hymn which begins with the line,

"From Greenland's icy mountains, from India's coral strands", and later contains the couplet,

"In vain with lavish kindness the gifts of God are strown;
The Heathen in his blindness bows down to wood and stone".

It is impossible to gauge the severity of cultural shock which

Vivekananda must have experienced, suddenly to move from his own ancient civilization into a pioneer nation, scarcely out of its swaddling clothes. At one level, he might genuinely admire the sheer energy and drive of the American people; at another, he was profoundly disappointed by their lack of staying power, when it came to real work in the spiritual field. They would seize avidly enough onto a new idea, but all too often, the novelty wore off when something else became the vogue. One of Vivekananda's American disciples, Leon Landsberg, said of his countrymen, that there was "no theory so absurd, no doctrine so irrational, no claim so extravagant, no fraud so transparent" which could not find a ready market. According to Landsberg, "Hobgoblins, spooks, mahatmas, and new prophets were rising every day".

Fortunately, Vivekananda, with his excellent English and ready wit, was more than able to cope with this fairground atmosphere, but, at the same time, it took its toll on his nervous energy, and he often became disenchanted with the frenetic, money-grabbing ambience of Western capitalism. He also found the constant attacks by "orthodox inimical Christians" both saddening and frustrating, and his lectures should be read in the knowledge that he was forever struggling to make himself understood to audiences often less than sympathetic to the ideas he was putting forward.

Perhaps the greatest adjustment Vivekananda had to make during his stay in the States was in pace and tempo of living. He was always making fun of the American habit of rushing here and there, and never hurried himself. If he was late for a lecture or failed to keep to schedule, it was a matter of complete indifference to him. Indeed, when he first reached America, he was all too apt to slip into a state of meditation and quite forget where he was or what he was supposed to be doing. Sister Nivedita (Vivekananda's most celebrated woman disciple, Margaret Noble) recalled that initially "it was no uncommon thing for him to be carried two or three times round a tram-circuit". She added that he was very much ashamed of these lapses, however, and worked hard to overcome them. Indeed, he worked to such effect, that he became as alert and wide-awake as the world in which he found himself, and yet never lost the majestic calm which was his hallmark. When someone once expostulated with him for having no idea of time, he said in reply, "You live in time; we live in eternity!"

As Vivekananda toured America, he gave lectures at the prodigious rate of twelve to fourteen a week. No attempt will be made here to outline what he was saying in those lectures—that will be dealt with in the second part of this book. For the moment, the focus will be on his technique as a public speaker and some of the difficulties with which he had to contend.

He had made his début at the Parliament of Religions, and, with practice, his lecturing style became more and more polished. He always spoke extempore and never used notes, varying his pace and content to suit his audience; he never forgot the needs and limitations of his listeners, and that no doubt was why they listened to him so attentively. As he wrote in a letter to India in 1895, "to put the Hindu ideas into English and then make out of dry philosophy, and intricate mythology and queer startling psychology, a religion which shall be easy, simple and popular and at the same time meet the requirements of the highest minds—it is a task only those can understand who have attempted it".

Vivekananda never bored his audiences, although he sometimes upset them; he was a superb actor and mimic, and his style was colloquial, fresh and forceful. Newspaper reports refer to his "affable manner" and "the slow, soft, quiet, unimpassioned musical voice embodying its thought with all the power and fire of the most vehement physical utterance". In short, he was a wow.

One evening, in a small town hotel, when he found his energies beginning to wane, Vivekananda accused his Master of putting him in an impossible position. How could he be expected to think of new things to say to yet another audience? It was ridiculous! He'd had enough of it. But then, to his amazement, he heard a voice, and it was the voice of Ramakrishna speaking loud and clear in his native Bengali, telling him precisely what to say the next day. Even more remarkable was the enquiry the following morning from the guest who had been sleeping in the room next door, who said that he had been wakened in the middle of the night by the conversation which the Swami had been having with his friend, who was presumably Indian, as they had been speaking in a language which was quite incomprehensible. Vivekananda managed somehow to fend off the question, but the nocturnal interchanges continued, and he came to rely completely for his material on this overnight preparation. Often enough, the information came in the form of a voice, as it had on the first occasion, but sometimes, he saw pictures which illustrated a train of ideas, and all he had to do was to use them as cues in the lectures the next day. Frequently what reached him was quite new and unfamiliar, and he came to enjoy his lectures as much as his listeners, because the material was as fresh to him as to them.

People who asked silly questions were quickly put in their place. The man who asked if Vivekananda had ever seen an elemental was told, "Oh yes, we have them in India for breakfast". And as for the babies being thrown to the crocodiles . . . oh yes, his mother had taken him down to the Ganges all right, but he was such a fat little baby the crocodiles refused to swallow him. "Whenever I think badly about being such a fat monk, I think of how I was saved from the crocodiles and am comforted."

Less amusing were the brushes with Christian propagandists, who did everything in their power to discredit Vivekananda and invariably took refuge in abuse rather than argument. For them, it was impossible to imagine a man for whom women and money had simply ceased to be a temptation, and they tried to fabricate scandalous stories, even going as far as to send young women to seduce him. As Marie Louise Burke makes so clear in her *New Discoveries*, to every narrow mind

Vivekananda was a bête noire to be eliminated at any cost. Apart from malicious gossip, there was even an attempt to put him out of the way altogether by poisoning his coffee, but this failed because the Swami had a presentiment that all was not well, and left the coffee untasted.

Vivekananda was accused of being "a teacher of deadly error" and those who followed him were assured that they would surely enter the fiery pit. The Swami in his turn did not mince matters, but roundly declared that Americans were Christians only in name, and that it was high time they went back to the teachings of Jesus. "You are beasts! beasts! I say, with the morals of a tom-cat . . ." Little wonder that he emptied whole halls!

What Vivekananda was saying was fatal to orthodox belief, as taught by the Christian teachers. Somewhat naturally, the said teachers did not appreciate having their noses put out of joint, and conflict was inevitable.

But it would be quite misleading to leave the impression that Vivekananda's tour of America was a running battle and no more. With the exception of the missionaries and the "church-women" (a chilling phrase!), the Swami found his hosts hospitable, kind-hearted, generous and good-natured. They loved him and he loved them, and he felt as if he were one of them. He particularly appreciated the American preparedness to accept a man for what he was, without any question being asked about his peculiarities, "If a man is a man, that is enough, and they take him into their hearts, and that is one thing I have never seen in any other country in the world." The women enormously impressed him, and he found them far more cultivated than the men; the latter were fully occupied with making money and had no time for the frills of education and culture. Letters to people like Mrs. Ole Bull, the Hale sisters and Josephine MacLeod, all bear witness to the beautiful relationships with women which Vivekananda was able to establish. He kept romance at bay by making his women-friends call him "father" or "brother" and not allowing them to come near him with any other feeling. With them, it was possible to enter into dialogue at the deepest level, and apart from admiring "their broad and liberal minds", he felt deeply grateful to them for their kindness and consideration at all times during his stay.

For a few months in 1895, he was able temporarily to withdraw from the clamour of public lecturing to a small island on the St. Lawrence River—Thousand Island Park. Here, he and twelve men and women, who had felt drawn to join him, enjoyed a blissful period of discussion and meditation, and Vivekananda felt at his best because he had at last found a faithful few who were really prepared to take him as their teacher. Josephine MacLeod said afterwards that it was as if he made them realize that they were in eternity, and she thought that nothing revealed his heart as those days did. One of the students at Thousand Island Park was Dr. Wright of Cambridge, known affectionately as Dokie; after sitting at Vivekananda's feet for many hours, he said, "Well, Swami, it all amounts to this in the end, doesn't it? I *am* Brahman, I *am* the Absolute." "Yes, Dokie," came the reply, "you are Brahman, you are the Absolute, in the real essence of your being."

But after that, whenever the doctor approached, Vivekananda would say, "Here comes Brahman!", gently reminding Dokie that there is an enormous gap between grasping an idea mentally, and actually experiencing it as a reality. Vivekananda knew well enough how mortally attached Westerners are to their sense of being separate individuals with distinct identities, and he would mock those who were so afraid of losing their "in-di-vid-u-al-i-ty", by exclaiming, "Why, you are not individuals yet! When you know God, you will be."

What no one could escape, who met Vivekananda, was the sense of immense power which beamed out from him. At one moment he might be laughing uproariously at one of his favourite jokes (and how he loved jokes!), but the next it was as if he cast aside the layer of consciousness in which he was enjoying himself, and the sheer force of his presence made itself felt. As one disciple graphically put it, "He had the faculty of literally annihilating one if he chose"; indeed, one man had to rest in bed for three days, suffering from nervous exhaustion, after a meeting with the Swami.

The American lectures were very fully and accurately recorded, and this was entirely due to an Englishman named J. J. Goodwin, who took down the Swami's words in shorthand, and later typed the material out for publication. A court-stenographer, with a speed of two hundred words a minute, Goodwin demanded a high salary for his services when he was hired in the first instance. However, after a week of listening to Vivekananda, he refused to take any more money, saying that if the Swami was prepared to give his life, the least he could do was to give his service.

And certainly, Vivekananda *did* give his life to his audiences in the States; by 1896, he was desperately in need of rest. He told Mary Hale that he would like to become dumb for some years and not talk at all, but more work remained to be done in England and India, and his talking days were by no means over. Marie Louise Burke has the truth of the matter when she writes that Vivekananda did not lecture—he gave. For the first sixteen months he lit the fire of spirituality, and for the next sixteen months, he left the legacy of spiritual and philosophical knowledge by which the fire might be fed in the years to come. "Almost a whole nation had barked after the Swamiji", wrote Miss Burke, "but he had strode on unperturbed, chastising where it was necessary with one or two well-directed blows, awakening and quickening the minds of thousands, and bestowing his blessings upon friend and foe alike."

In an absurdly short space of time, Vivekananda had visited every city from the Atlantic coast down to the Mississippi; he had lectured to audiences ranging from cowboys to university professors, and the Vedanta Society of New York had come into existence. After only a few short months in America, he had seen that if India's strength lay in spirituality, the New World had much to teach the East in terms of social conscience. "As regards spirituality, the Americans are far inferior to us, but their society is far superior to ours" he wrote home to an Indian friend. "We will teach them our spirituality and assimilate what is best in their society." Or, as he once pointedly asked an audience, "Your religion helps you to build Ferris wheels and Eiffel towers, but does it aid you in the development of your inner lives?"

Vivekananda realized what has since become progressively more apparent, that Western man, behind his mask of cheerfully brisk efficiency, is basically frightened and unable to find real peace of mind. In E. M. Forster's phrase, "telegrams and anger" are the cover for "panic and emptiness". As Vivekananda toured the United States, he found a social life characterized by hysteria and hypocrisy, but behind the laughter he heard a wail of dismay which ended in a sob. "I hate this world," he wrote to Mary Hale, "I hate this dream, this horrible nightmare, with its churches and chicaneries, its books and blackguardisms, its fair faces and false hearts, its howling righteousness on the surface and utter hollowness beneath, and above all, its sanctified shopkeeping." In India, men begged for bread, but in America they cried out for spiritual nourishment and this was an appeal which went straight to the Swami's heart, for all his annoyance with the "churches and chicaneries". He saw no alternative but to give and not to count the cost: the results of that stupendous gift can never be estimated, but it is enough to recognize that the effects of his mission to America have been felt ever since. The amazing Mr. Kananda had done his bit.

Chapter Eight

SAHIBS REDISCOVERED

"In England of course they are gentlemen." (Vivekananda)

One day Vivekananda was taking a walk through some fields in England with a Miss Henrietta Müller and another man, when suddenly a bull came charging towards them. The man incontinently fled, while Miss Müller ran until she collapsed to the ground in exhaustion. Vivekananda, realising that there was little he could do to help the lady, stood in front of her with folded arms facing the oncoming juggernaut. He admitted afterwards that he thought his last moment had come and his mind was occupied with calculating how far the bull would be able to toss him with those wicked-looking horns. However, the animal stopped short of the impassive figure of the Swami: man and beast stared at each other for a few seconds, and then, with a bewildered look on his great face, the bull lifted his head, slowly wheeled round and beat a surly retreat.

Happily Vivekananda's confrontations with John Bull on his visits to Great Britain were less nerve-wracking than that encounter, but nevertheless, he first set foot on English soil with considerable misgivings. Soon after leaving India, he had given vent to his hatred of the race which had "sucked the last drop of our blood for their own pleasures", and he had gone on to express a great longing to be shot by the English government. "It would be the first nail in their coffin, and my death would run through the land like wild fire." For him, after all, the English governing India were the hated overlords, who, with their perspiring beefsteak complexions and uncouth, lubberly ways had done little to earn the respect or affection of the subject race. There were, of course, exceptions, as the Swami would have been the first to admit, but the outburst quoted above, indicates the depth and violence of his feelings against

British rule. What galled him above all else was the attitude and behaviour of the missionaries, who felt entitled to ride roughshod over customs and beliefs of which they had no understanding, in order to bring a heathen people to Christ.

Hence, when Vivekananda came to London for the first time in 1895, he was not favourably predisposed towards England and the English. It is a mark of his fundamental fairness and honesty, that he revised his opinions completely after meeting the Sahibs on their home ground. For one thing he was delighted to find that, apart from a few Anglo-Indians, the English had no colour prejudice. In the States, he had been turned away from hotels on account of his colour, but in the Britain of the 1890s, a dark skin was accepted without demur, and the Swami was spared the humiliation of being hooted at in the streets. Sometimes, indeed, he even wondered whether his face had turned white!

It was from England that Vivekananda obtained his most outstanding disciples: Goodwin has already been mentioned, and later additions included Mr. and Mrs. Sevier, who regarded the Swami both as a son and a teacher, and of course, Margaret Noble, later known as Sister Nivedita. These were the people who were to return with Vivekananda to India and do so much to launch the Ramakrishna Mission and the Ashrama at Mayavati in the Himalayas. (It is interesting to note, incidentally, that the trio of writers who have done so much in the twentieth century to further the cause of Vedanta—Aldous Huxley, Gerald Heard and Christopher Isherwood—were all English, although they chose latterly to live in California).

If Vivekananda found John Bull somewhat dull-witted when it came to implanting new ideas, once something had really penetrated that thick skull, then it was there forever. The Swami discerned "a deep spring of feeling" in the English, despite their care never to show emotion if they could possibly help it, and he was therefore prepared to forgive them for being rather slow on the uptake. He confessed to Mary and Harriet Hale in a letter that his ideas about the English had been revolutionised, and went on to describe them as "steady, sincere to the backbone, with great depths of feeling—only with a crust of stoicism on the surface; if that is broken, you have your man". He felt that they had solved the secret of obedience without slavish cringing, and there was considerable freedom with a great preparedness to be law-abiding. As in the States, he was impressed by the women, although he saw that Englishwomen were less emancipated than their American sisters, and generally had a narrower sphere in society. The overall change in his attitude towards the English was summed up in his remark to the Hindus of Calcutta, when he returned to India, "No one ever landed on English soil feeling more hatred in his heart for a race than I did for the English . . . there is none among you loves the English people more than I do."

In Britain, Vivekananda was able to shake off the image of entertainer and magician, and settle down to some really serious and effective teaching. Publicity was considerable less brash than in the States, and reports about him which appeared in the newspapers were objective, courteous and civilized. An interviewer from the *Sunday Times*, for example, asked the Swami if his teaching could be described as a system of comparative religion, to which Vivekananda replied that it might convey a more definite idea to call it "the kernel of all forms of religion, stripping from them the non-essential, and laying stress on that which is the real basis". This, of course, was really accurate reporting, and I am charmed by the same interviewer who said a little later in the same article, "It sounds just a little vague and remote from practical life, that the Divine is within everything but covered. One can't be looking for it all the time."

Vivekananda did not hesitate to denounce the commercial prosperity, bloody wars, and religious intolerance of the West, but in England, he was not attacked and persecuted by churchmen or anyone else for his views; on the contrary, he enjoyed the friendship and support of many leading clerics and aristocrats. The people who attended his lectures were, in the main, both highly bred and highly educated, and were prepared to listen thoughtfully to what was laid before them. Margaret Noble, in fact, first met Vivekananda in a West End drawing room, where he was regaling a group of fashionable ladies sitting cross-legged on the floor. Because he was talking to bright and perceptive audiences, the Swami was able to speak at a different level from before, and his London lectures on maya are justly praised as being amongst his best.

Whereas in the States, Vivekananda had tried to make money with his lectures, in England he found it preferable to avoid any dealing with money whatsoever, refusing even voluntary contributions. He felt that he had fallen victim to profiteers in the earlier part of his career in the West, and also believed that spiritual power must inevitably be lost, if there is worry about whether one is making a profit or not.

Initially, one of the Swami's most reliable friends in England was E. T. Sturdy, who had studied Sanskrit and had even practised a certain amount of yoga in the Himalayas. A letter to Josephine MacLeod in September, 1895, told of Vivekananda's safe arrival in London and his subsequent journey to Reading where Mr. and Mrs. Sturdy provided him with accommodation. The tone of the letter is cheerful, saying how much more at home he felt in England than he had anywhere else out of India. "The English people know us, we know them." Mrs. Sturdy was likened to an angel, and the house at Reading delighted the visitor in both its beauty and comfort.

But the idyll was short-lived, because the Swami later recalled his stay at Reading with horror, where he was fed with boiled cabbage and boiled potatoes and boiled rice and boiled lentils, three times a day, with Mrs Sturdy's "curses for sauce all the time". Apparently the lady's angelic nature did not survive for long after the arrival of her foreign visitor, who had the distressing habit of smoking "all over the house". Reading between the lines, it looks as if the Sturdys were puritans at heart, yoga or no yoga in the Himalayas, and they took the Swami to task for his "luxurious" tastes. By late 1899,

Vivekananda could no longer look for support from them, and this saddened him a good deal, although he attributed the rift to karma which could not be avoided.

Margaret Noble, on the other hand, proved to be a tower of strength. She was running her own school in Wimbledon and playing a leading role in cultural circles when she first met Vivekananda. Although not immediately convinced by the Swami's teachings, she was deeply impressed by the breadth of his religious views, by the freshness of his approach, and, most of all, by his transparent integrity. She was ripe for a spiritual awakening and quickly divined that where others talked of ways and means, Vivekananda knew how to light a fire. In her book, *The Master as I Saw Him*, Sister Nivedita gives a unique picture of the Swami in the last few years of his life.

Vivekananda's work in England was more satisfying to him than his work in America, and he felt it was more likely to last and bear fruit. It is difficult to gauge now just how deeply Vedanta has established itself in Britain; so many "spiritual" groups of every conceivable kind have proliferated in the last decade. For me the Advaita philosophy is the most coherent and intelligible explanation of truth that I have come across, and I believe it must inevitably form the basis of the universal religion which is emerging at the moment. Vivekananda's hope was to imbue individuals with his ideas and to encourage them to express them to others in their own way. He was not averse to modifications of the teachings and never insisted on any hard and fast dogmas. Writing as I do in an England sadly less admirable than it would appear to have been at the turn of the century (are we still "steady, sincere to the backbone, with great depths of feeling", I wonder?), it is nevertheless my conviction that Vivekananda's lively and inspired approach to God can profitably be considered at a time in our history when so much lies in the balance. The truth or otherwise of a teaching, is less a matter of whether it stands the test of time, than whether it is equally valid at *all* times. What I find so attractive about Vivekenanda is that what he says is not tied to any particular era; it's either eternally true or eternally false. But before we embark on a consideration of these ideas, it remains to tell the story of the Swami's last years.

Chapter Nine

DEPARTURE

"If a man knows that he is He, why should he hunger for a body?"
(Brihadaranyaka Upanishad)

At the turn of the century, Vivekananda was to make a final visit to the United States, this time to California, and apart from his stays in England, he saw a good deal of Europe and the Middle East on different occasions. Before he left India for the first time in 1893, he had passionately believed in the value of travel, as the only way to discover what was really going on in the world at large. By 1900, he had seen Paris and Berlin, climbed the Alps, attended High Mass at St. Peter's, Rome, and visited Vienna, Constantinople and Athens, amongst other places. It was typical of him to start learning French in his late thirties to have better access to European culture. He declared that the main effect of all this globe-trotting was to make him much less quick to find fault with others than he had been in his youth. As he remarked to an American audience, "I have travelled not a little in my life; I have kept my eyes open; and the more I go about, the more my mouth is closed. I have no criticism to offer." This was not because his famous discrimination had deserted him, but because he had come to full realisation of the truth that he had so frequently stressed in his lectures—that verily, all is one, that behind the astonishing diversity of life in the universe, lies an underlying unity.

"O lovers, O lovers, it is time to abandon the world,
The drum of departure reaches my spiritual ear from heaven"
wrote the Sufi mystic Jalal'ud-Din Rumi, and the leitmotif of this chapter will be the muffled beat of that "drum of departure", culminating in Vivekananda's death in 1902. As early as 1897, the Swami felt that his task was done and estimated that he had only a few years of life left. In fact, much

strenuous work was to be accomplished in those last five years, and Vivekananda's body—stigmatized by its owner as "this cage of flesh and blood"—was not finally dropped until he knew without the least doubt, that he had done what was required of him. Just before his death, he said that the shadow of a big tree does not let the smaller trees grow up, and he must therefore go to make room for his successors, the latter-day Vivekanandas, of whom there would be "thousands and millions"! The fact that he himself was shortly to die didn't matter in the slightest, because he reckoned he had given the world enough to be getting on with for the next fifteen hundred years.

Apart from prophesying his own end, Vivekananda made other prognostications, which events have proved to be remarkably accurate. He said that India would be free of the British yoke in fifty years, and suggested that China and Russia would be the great powers of the future. In more general terms, he likened Europe to a volcano which could not fail to erupt unless the fires were extinguished "by a flood of spirituality". He envisaged the coming of "a huge spiritual tide" and believed that the religion of future enlightened humanity would be Advaitism. But he was not at all clear how long it would take for the whole of mankind to become spiritual, recognising that the old superstitions must first die out, which would probably take an unconscionable time. His hope lay with Westerners who, he believed, would come to the truth of the Advaita philosophy more quickly than Orientals; the East, he felt, had almost exhausted itself in formulating the idea and in producing a few outstanding cases of individual realisation, whereas in the West, there seemed more likelihood of the idea becoming widely accepted. The key to Vivekananda's thinking in this direction lies in his statement that "the only universal religion in the world is the amity of religions", and he conceived of a new order of humanity who would be sincere believers in God, and who would care nothing for the world. Such people would have all the breadth and depth of *real* spirituality, because their love would give them no alternative. It was a noble vision of the shape of things to come, and we shall be considering in a later chapter just how far it can be said to have come to pass.

In January, 1897, Vivekananda landed in Ceylon at Colombo to meet with an extraordinary welcome from his countrymen. In America he had sometimes had difficulty in being admitted to a decent hotel, and had suffered considerable persecution from bigots and fanatics of one kind and another. On his arrival back home, he was greeted as the Man of the Hour, as a spiritual giant, and princes vied to draw his carriage. Vivekananda was delighted to find that, for Hindus, a hero was neither warrior, artist, nor statesman: for them, the sannyasin epitomised what they most admired. After a tremendous reception at Colombo, the Swami moved on to the north coast of Ceylon and there the people of Jaffna, in their welcoming address, expressed their indebtedness to Vivekananda "for making the people of the West know the catholicity of our religion and for impressing upon the minds of the savants of the West the truth that there are more things in the philosophy of the Hindus than are dreamt of in the philosophy of the West". At Pamban, the Swami told his countrymen that the Western nations were looking to India for spiritual help and that a great moral obligation rested on India's sons to fit themselves for the stupendous task of enlightening the whole world.

As Vivekananda travelled up into the heart of India, he began to outline his hopes for the future, of a marriage between Eastern insight and Western outlook, so that a safe course might be steered between "the Scylla of old orthodoxy and the Charybdis of modern European civilization". He ridiculed the "kitchen" religion which too many Indians mistook for the path to holiness, and was even more scathing in his attacks on "don't touchism"; his one ambition was to awaken his people to the situation and their duty, and to that end he was prepared to broadcast his message from one end of India to the other. The country must be deluged with spiritual ideas and flooded with new expertise.

The Swami did not flatter his listeners: they were compared with "downtrodden worms", and words could not express his disgust for what he conceived to be their lack of stamina. Rather than moon about reading *The Gita*, they would be better employed playing football. How different an approach from the one he had adopted in America and England! He was never fool enough to preach the same message to audiences with different needs, and I share Christopher Isherwood's delight in the way that Vivekananda was eternally changing sides when he was speaking to different people, because "he was really on everybody's side".

Like Martin Luther King, Vivekananda had a dream, a dream which he wished all who heard him to make a reality—a dream that the world must be conquered by India, not with hatred and destruction, but with love, so that death should have no more dominion, and a new co-operation and understanding would at last enable men to live together, "in wisdom and in truth".

Vivekananda railed against his countrymen who could not even manufacture a needle, and told them they were in no position to criticise the English until they could learn to be more practical, and to work together as a group without squabbling. And so he urged his "brave boys" to learn to get things properly organised and to adopt business-like methods. Above all, they must be completely straightforward and honest in their dealings with others. "No shilly-shally, no esoteric blackguardism, no secret humbug, nothing should be done in a corner." With characteristic exuberance, Vivekananda said he was ready to undergo a hundred thousand rebirths to train up a single man.

The tendency of the Hindu, in the face of difficulty, was to take refuge in the idea of karma, seen as an inexorable and unalterable law of cause and effect, which seemingly meant one could not hope to defy the inevitable. Much play was also made of the notion of maya, that miasma of ignorance which prevents one from seeing things as they really are. Consequently, it was all too easy to dismiss life on earth as an "illusion", in which the wisest and best policy was to do nothing. Vivekananda was infuriated by this kind of thinking; not that he quarrelled with the doctrines of karma and maya, quite the reverse,—but he hated people to use metaphysics as an excuse for laziness and irresponsibility. The following conversation between the Swami and a disciple perfectly illustrates what Vivekananda was up against:

Disciple: But, sir, what will be the use of undertaking such works? Is not death stalking behind?

Swamiji: Fie upon you! If you die, you will die but once. Why will you die every minute of your life by constantly harping on death like a coward?

Disciple: All right, sir, I may not think of death, but what good will come of any kind of work in this evanescent world?

Swamiji: My boy, when death is inevitable, is it not better to die like heroes than as sticks and stones? And what is the use of living a day or two more in this transitory world? It is better to wear out than to rust out—specially for the sake of doing the least good to others.

Disciple: It is true, sir. I beg pardon for troubling you so much.

Vivekananda's policy for India was initially to inject enough self-respect into his people, to enable them to stand up for themselves. In the West, he had stressed the need for remembering God in the midst of a fiercely competitive, frenetically active society; in India, he admitted that knowledge of Brahman was obviously the ultimate goal, but absorption in the divine did not exonerate one from hard work. He realised the obscenity of telling starving people that pleasure is a form of bondage. No one could possibly see any sense in that idea, until he had eaten decent food, worn attractive clothes, and, in short, known what it was to be self-indulgent. Bhoga must precede yoga: which freely translated, means that until you've had a good time, union with the divine is not to be attempted.

The seal of the Ramakrishna Math and Mission which appears on the front cover of this book consists of a swan resting on a lotus in ruffled water. The swan's head is silhouetted against a rising sun, and the whole seal is bordered by a snake whose head and tail meet at the top. Vivekananda explained that the snake stands for mysticism, the sun for knowledge, while the worked-up waters symbolise activity and the lotus represents love. The swan is the soul in the midst of all.

In 1898, Calcutta was stricken by a plague and observers were astonished to see a band of monks accompanied by a white woman going about visiting every home, discovering who needed help, tending the sick, removing the dead and clearing accumulated rubbish and filth. Here, in India, for the first time since Buddha, organised monasticism was in action fired by a tradition of selfless service. Vivekananda's idea was to create a new order of sannyasins, who would renounce the world, but would not thereby opt out of it. The Math at Belur became the headquarters of the Ramakrishna Order and before long, the monks were out in the field doing work of all kinds. Preachers went to different parts of India to revive interest in Vedanta; others were despatched to England, America, Australia and New Zealand; and wherever famine or disease broke out, attempts were made by the Order to relieve distress.

Since then the tendency has been for the Order to concentrate on medical and educational work in India, and to serve cultural and spiritual interests in the West. In this, the trend is, of course, exactly in line with what Vivekananda himself had done. The monks of the Ramakrishna Order are world citizens and in their constant fight against social injustices, they are entirely above any limitations of creed, race or language; dedicated to human welfare, and committed to the idea of world unity, they are, like their founder, involved in mankind.

In the May-June issue of *Vedanta for East and West* for 1976, an article by Joseph Temple tells of his visit to India, where he saw a large general hospital under the auspices of the Ramakrishna Mission, and later the excellent educational work at Narendrapur. Of the latter, he writes:

"The work done here is absolutely magnificent. Apart from general, technical and vocational education of about 850 pupils in general studies and about 350 in advanced studies, there is education of 100 or more blind boys in Braille and also music and handicrafts. There is also a farming training course. But what most impressed me was the training of fully and partially blind men and boys in a machine shop, working on capstan lathes, drilling machines, etc. Narendrapur and the work the Mission does there made a great impact on me."

Vivekananda's other great innovation was the creation of the Ashrama at Mayavati, situated fifty miles from Almora, 6300 feet up into the Himalayas. From the start, Mayavati was concerned entirely with Advaitism and there was therefore no worship of images, pictures or symbols of God. When Vivekananda discovered that pictures of Ramakrishna were being used for devotional purposes, he strictly forbade this practice, not from lack of respect for his Master, but because, in the last resort, Reality can have no expression in external form. Mr. and Mrs. Sevier worked at Mayavati, and after her husband's death, Mrs. Sevier stayed on for many years at the Ashrama. In January 1901, Vivekananda could write with enthusiasm to Mrs. Ole Bull that "this place is very, very beautiful, and they have made it simply exquisite." A photograph of Mayavati is used on the cover of the present edition of Vivekananda's *Complete Works*, and certainly I hope one day to pay the Ashrama a visit.

Of course, the launching of the Ramakrishna Mission, the founding of Mayavati and so on, involved an enormous amount of work, and Vivekananda bore the brunt of the administrative side of all this. His natural tendency to a life of scholarship and meditation had to be sternly kept in check, and although he recognised in 1897 that he was at the very height of his destiny, he longed for quietness and peace. He compared his lot with that of a beast being driven to a slaughter-house, hastily nibbling a bite of grass on the roadside as he is driven along by the whip. But he never spared himself and we are told by

Nivedita that "he had a whole-hearted contempt for what he regarded as squeamishness or mawkishness". More and more towards the end, he stressed the need to come to terms with what he called the Terrible. He realised that all struggle was pointless, and yet, at the same time, it was necessary: the only route to heaven lay through hell. Death must be welcomed, he insisted, and this had nothing to do with cowardice, weakness or suicidal tendencies, but was rather "the welcome of the strong man, who has sounded everything to its depths, and *knows* that there is no alternative".

In a remarkably moving letter written to "Joe" (Josephine MacLeod) on 18 April, 1900, he said that he regretted nothing that he had done, and he rejoiced at the death of the "old man" which released him from the roles of guru and leader, so that only "the boy, the student, the servant" was left behind. Later in the same letter he wrote, "Behind my work was ambition, behind my love was personality, behind my purity was fear, behind my guidance, the thirst for power! Now they are vanishing, and I drift."

Vivekananda's health declined rapidly in the last years, and he succumbed to successive attacks of diabetes, asthma and dropsy. His mind retained its usual brilliance, however, and his memory was as formidable as ever. A disciple found him reading Volume XI of the 25 Volume set of the *Encyclopaedia Britannica* which had recently arrived in India from England. The Swami was working his way systematically through the volumes, and when questioned on the ones he had read, was able to answer all he was asked, often quoting large passages verbatim.

More important, from a spiritual point of view, was Vivekananda's attainment to that peace that passeth all understanding. As he wrote to Mary Hale, his intention now was "to see things as they are, everything in that peace, perfect in its way". For so long he had preached the theory, "but oh joy! Mary, my dear sister, I am realising it now every day".

Increasingly the Swami found the presence of worldly people

distasteful to him: a horrible stench of lust seemed to cling to their clothes and bodies. Simply to be incarnate was very hell. He found his duties as Abbot of Belur more and more burdensome, and latterly withdrew as much as possible from the entanglement of administrative worries. The beat of the drum of departure quickened into a roll rising to a crescendo, as Death stalked closer and closer throughout 1902.

On Friday, 4 July, he got up extremely early and meditated for three hours in the chapel, after shutting the windows and bolting the doors (quite against his normal practice). Later in the morning he was overheard to say to himself, "If there were another Vivekananda, then he would have understood what this Vivekananda has done! And yet—how many Vivekanandas shall be born in time!"

He ate a good lunch and taught Sanskrit grammar to young disciples for three hours in the afternoon. At 7 p.m. he retired to his room with strict instructions that he was not to be disturbed. After an hour's meditation, he called his attendant and asked for all the windows to be opened, after which he lay down on his bed.

For what followed, I cannot do better than give Swami Nikhilananda's account:

"At the end of an hour his hands trembled a little and he breathed once very deeply. There was a silence for a minute or two, and again he breathed in the same manner. His eyes became fixed in the centre of his eyebrows, his face assumed a divine expression, and eternal silence fell . . . The great ecstasy took place at ten minutes past nine. Swami Vivekananda passed away at the age of thirty-nine years, five months, and twenty-four days, thus fulfilling his own prophecy: "I shall not live to be forty years old'."

Doctors could not agree on the cause of death, some attributing it to heart failure, others to brain haemorrhage. For myself, I would agree with the verdict that this was the type of the Free Man's death: Vivekananda was not overtaken by death, but left his body of his own volition.

At the funeral pyre the next day, Nivedita was beside herself with grief and wept like a child at the passing of her Lord. But it fell to Nivedita, above all others of Vivekananda's Western disciples, to give her work and talent to her Master's beloved India.

Visitors to modern India will find a Vivekananda Bridge in Calcutta and a statue of the Swami by the "Gateway to India" at Bombay. (This monumental Gateway incidentally was built to celebrate the visit of George V and Queen Mary in 1912; the statue of Vivekananda was not put up till 1971). There is, besides, the worldwide network of the Ramakrishna Mission. But the most heartening legacy of Vivekananda lies in what he said shortly before that "great ecstasy", when he made a promise, and the promise was that after casting off his body like a worn-out garment, he would not cease to work, but would inspire men everywhere, "until the world shall know that it is one with God"

It is a mistake to see Vivekananda as no more than a great patriot, who fought to create a better future for his people, and indeed for all humanity. Assuredly, he was involved in mankind, and certainly he fought as few have fought to make the world a better place to live in, but he knew that the world did not really *need* him, and was fond of saying that there is as little hope of straightening out the world, as there is of straightening out a dog's curly tail. All that he accomplished, he attributed to God, and however much he may have done in the way of social reform, his real concern at all times and with all people was to give them the chance to be free. No matter how Utopian society might be, in the last resort, freedom for Vivekananda was an inner quality, and could only be won by each person for himself. His recommendations on how to be free will be our concern for the remainder of this book.

PART TWO:

THE MESSAGE

Chapter Ten

THE CIRCUS

"We see the world as we are." (Vivekananda)

Of Human Bondage—Somerset Maugham stole the phrase from Spinoza, and I was tempted to use the same words as the title for this chapter. But Vivekananda put me in mind of the idea of the circus, with its overtones of absurdity and excitement. Can there be anything more transient than a circus? The "Big Top", the performing animals, the clowns, the strong man, and the rest: all here today and gone tomorrow. An earnest lady once told the Swami that she saw life on earth as being tantamount to going to school, to which he replied with a snort, "Who told you that the world is a school? . . . This world is a circus, and we are clowns come to tumble."

"Why do we tumble, Swami?" asked the lady.

"Because we like to tumble. When we get tired of tumbling, we quit."

This picture of falling about, and getting nowhere, is a perfect illustration of our failure to see what life is all about. As Vivekananda wrote to another lady in 1899, "This toy world would not be here, this play could not go on, if we were knowing players. We must play blindfolded."

In any attempt to discuss bondage, several difficulties arise, not least the fact that many people don't see themselves as prisoners at all, but believe they are free to do as they please. To talk to them in terms of the dungeon of the ego and so forth is a waste of time. Others, on the other hand, may acknowledge the fact of human bondage, but take the gloomy view that there is no way out, and therefore grit their teeth to endure to the end as best they may. These latter are the stoics.

Some few, however, realize their plight and this realization makes them quite desperate, so much so indeed that they develop the will, and find the way to escape. The word "escapist" has a negative ring to it: it suggests someone running away from something he can't face. There can, however, be situations which are so manifestly intolerable, that the most sensible thing to do *is* to escape. For me, it is clear that we are "cribbed, cabined and confined", but no matter how escape-proof our particular Colditz may appear to be, we can, like the redoubtable Houdini, break our bonds and be free. But, of course, it should never be forgotten that Houdini was an expert escapologist, and he took enormous risks.

We live in a culture which sets little store by spiritual disciplines. It is blandly assumed that life is not as bad as all that, provided that one has plenty of luck, decent health and not too much imagination. If it begins to dawn on anyone that all is not well, then the stock answer is to seek the anodyne of "amusement". There is no lack of diversions and entertainments to keep the wolves from the door: the wolves of insecurity and fear, of frustration and disappointment, of conflict and doubt. It has to be confessed that we are not always amused, as our well-filled mental hospitals bear witness. In wartime, the phenomenon of "battle fatigue" has frequently been remarked, when men are no longer able to cope with the horrors of active service, and opt out by developing such symptoms as hysterical blindness or deafness, or quite simply coming to the end of their quota of "moral fibre". Each person has his breaking point, and unless the pressure is lifted in time, collapse is inevitable.

Aldous Huxley coined the telling phrase of "God-eclipsing imbecilities" and suggested that "the imbecile within us is as radically God's enemy as the passionately purposeful maniac, with his insane cravings and aversions. Moreover, the imbecile remains at large and busy after the lunatic has been tamed or even destroyed". Huxley's cure for this ill was to drop "the habit of disquietude", and to empty the memory of the burdens of the past.

But it is pertinent to ask how we acquired this habit of

disquietude in the first place. What ails us? Vivekananda's answer was that we have bound ourselves by our own actions over many lifetimes, and what we are now is directly related to what we were in the past. This, of course, hinges on an acceptance of reincarnation as a matter of fact, rather than an Oriental fancy. For us of the West, the notion of having lived before is still treated with considerable scepticism, and often dismissed as a joke. People who claim to recall being Pharaoh, or being burnt at the stake, may get into the media, but they are usually presented as oddities, and great pains are taken to supply alternative explanations to that of reincarnation, such as genetic memory, psychic vestiges or plain fraud. In a recent radio interview, a man named Edward Ryall said that he had clear memories of his earlier life as one, John Fletcher, who died at the battle of Sedgemoor in 1685. Various pundits had been invited into the studio including an inquisitorial Professor of Psychology, who weighed in with the remark that "we have not the slightest evidence, even a single case, of a memory existing without a brain". Later a Mathematics Professor said that, for him, non-physical energy was a complete contradiction in terms: he could not conceive of memories which are transmitted non-physically. Eventually one professor gently suggested to his colleague that he'd got at least to leave his mind open, to be met by the acid comeback, "Not so open that my brain would fall out." So much for the wisdom of the West!

Much has been written about reincarnation and I shall not make any attempt to "prove" it in this book. It is one of those things that some people accept quite readily, partly because it answers so many difficulties about the apparent injustices of life, but mainly because it corresponds to an inner conviction based on experience. Plato spoke of amnesis or recollection, the doctrine that when we encounter "our" truth, it is instantly recognised as an old friend, strangely forgotten and overlooked, but now rediscovered. For me, reincarnation is like that. Although I cannot, like Edward Ryall, recall specific experiences, there is the undeniable assurance that I did not make my first appearance on this planet on June 28, 1935. To anyone who likes to have a case made out, this will amount to no more than personal whimsy. No matter. Vivekananda had no doubt that a time comes for all of us when we shall remember the innumerable times we had fathers and mothers, sons and daughters, husbands and wives, relatives and friends, wealth and power. Memories of success and failure, happiness and misery will all come crowding back: it will be overwhelming, and we can be glad that, by and large, the memories are withheld until we are strong enough to cope with them. Vivekananda himself was asked if he could remember his earlier lives; he said that he could, but refused to discuss any details.

The basic and crucial principle involved in reincarnation is that we learn from experience, and our evolution towards freedom is governed by the rate of this learning. Progress at times seems woefully slow, but it is encouraging to know that no one grinds to a complete halt. There is always movement, usually forward, but occasionally backwards; one has to be exceptionally evil to lose ground badly, and in the long run, no one is left behind. Apparent mistakes may be helps rather than hindrances, but of course, this does not mean that we can cheerfully behave selfishly and assume that it will all work out for the best. Any attempt to establish either one's own or anybody else's "spiritual quotient" is ill-advised, but it remains helpful to have an overall picture of how the evolution of the soul works.

Vivekananda never tired of saying that it is no good being defeatist: life may not be a bowl of cherries, but nor yet is it some appalling game of snakes and ladders, in which the fall of the dice is a complete fluke. He stated boldly that it was up to us to make our own futures, and we should always remember that each word, thought and deed, has its effect: the bad ones are ready to spring upon us later "like tigers", but the good ones are "ready with the power of a hundred thousand angels" to defend us always and forever. Truly, we reap as we sow.

As was suggested at the outset of this book, nothing can be attributed to chance—we simply get what we deserve, what we have drawn to ourselves. To be born on earth is a great privilege, because it is only here that we have the opportunity for spiritual growth. But, at the same time, incarnation *is* incarceration, and the yearning for freedom which we all experience is, in fact, the desire for that birth of the eternal which can only be accomplished after the death of the transient. Freud's notion of the "death wish" was not as far-fetched as some have thought, but it is doubtful whether the father of psycho-analysis would accept my interpretation of his theory!

To become free, we have to get beyond the finite, beyond all limitations, and the way to freedom, for most of us, lies in "making use of the bondages themselves to break those very bondages". Vivekananda described successive human lives in his celebrated metaphor of the whirlpool, "A current rushing down of its own nature falls into a hollow and makes a whirlpool, and, after running a little in that whirlpool, it emerges again in the form of the free current to go on unchecked." In a sense, whirlpools might seem like unnecessary delays in the journey of the soul—why not travel direct in the mainstream? But to be human is to err, and although we may feel trapped and entangled in apparent cul-de-sacs, somehow the Divine Comedy embraces all the divergencies and ensures that, at the end of the Cosmic Day, all shall be well. This should not be interpreted sentimentally, of course: while we are in the whirlpool, there is much to suffer, and we get buffeted about. But then that is the nature of whirlpools.

How can we make use of the bondages themselves to break those very bondages? Vivekananda was no friend of those who "chew the cud of unsatisfied desires" and evade life's challenges by refusing to meet them. At the beginning of the *Bhagavad-Gita*, Arjuna is overcome by despair and grief at the prospect of having to fight a civil war, but Krishna tells him that this is a cowardly attitude and it is essential to perform one's task in life, and to perform it without desire, that is, without any hope of reward. This is the famous doctrine of non-attachment, and it is this idea which is central to understanding the nature of bondage. For example, as I type these words, it is no good thinking all the time of the readers who may or may not one day look at them: even if no one ever reads this book, that doesn't matter an iota. What matters is the fact that I've been fired to write.

"We have got ourselves caught," said the Swami, "caught in the trap, and we will have to work out our freedom." This can only be done by ceasing to be influenced by outside agencies and becoming master of one's inner universe. It is axiomatic, for example, that anything which inspires fear must be faced and conquered. There is the tale of Vivekananda at Varanasi when he was beset by a horde of savage monkeys, and he started to run away from them. However, he paused in his flight when a loud voice called out, "Face the brutes!" and lo and behold, no sooner had he followed this advice than they stopped dead in their tracks and ran gibbering to the trees.

The gist of Vivekananda's ideas about bondage can be summarised thus:

The tendency in human life is to be at the mercy of what is without, and any attempt to change the outer, but ignore the inner, cannot hope to succeed. Hence, the Western conception of a welfare state does not get to the root cause of our malaise, but only copes with its symptoms. The worst sin is ignorance, particularly ignorance of one's own strength, and the hallmark of bondage is the belief that one is weak and cannot overcome whatever one encounters. This belief arises from the crippling assumption that we are limited beings who must look for help from outside. Such is our craving for external aid, that we are prepared to behave completely irresponsibly, provided we have the sanction of our "superiors". Leaders are welcomed because there is nothing people like to do more, than submit themselves to an authority which relieves them of the burden of personal decision. This leader may take the form of a man (as in the classic dictatorships), or of an organization: either way, the individual has his worries taken care of, and can find peace of mind in obeying orders and accepting doctrines which those set in authority deem appropriate. The authorities, incidentally, seldom believe what they tell the masses, at least not in so crass a form, but they find it expedient to have a set of slogans which can be easily absorbed by those under their control. Freedom can only be won by those who are prepared to be outlaws, and go their own way. That is why Vivekananda advised people to avoid entering any church: he thought it good to be born in a church, but bad to die in one. In other words, we need a structure and a scheme of things at the outset, but with spiritual growth, the forms inevitably become cramping and must be shed if we are to be able to breathe freely. "It is very good to be born within the limits of certain forms that help the little plant of spirituality, but if a man dies within the bounds of these forms, it shows that he has not grown, that there has been no development of the soul . . . liberty is the first condition of growth."

It is difficult to resist the temptation to "put others right", i.e. bring them down to our own level of understanding, and elevate our personal views into eternally and universally valid moral imperatives. And the reason for this disagreeable habit, is because each individual can only see his own universe, and "that universe is created with his bondage and goes away with his liberation, *although it remains for others who are in bondage*".

Have we not all had the experience of falling in love with an idea, later becoming disenchanted with it, and eventually despising those who succumb to the very charms which we used to find so irresistible? What was formerly so necessary to us, indeed amounted to a holy of holies, suddenly stands revealed as just one of those things, and it is hard to see others being silly enough to be taken in as well. This goes some way towards explaining the sourness of elderly schoolmasters, who wince at each new generation being as gullible and naive as the last; great spiritual teachers, on the other hand, are able to view mankind's childishness without rancour.

Vivekananda, therefore, unlike Jonathan Swift, did not dismiss humanity as Lilliputians, whose tiny cavortings are fit subject only for satire. He strove to explain that pathetic craving for happiness which dogs us from our first thinking moments, "If only I won the pools, then . . .", "If only I could go to bed with so-and-so, then . . ." If only, if only—that endless litany of wants, which we chant unceasingly under our breath, and which, when the need arises to a crescendo, we shout shamelessly from the housetops.

But it is no good simply being told that desire is the father of misery, that "if the power to satisfy our desires is increased in arithmetical progression, the power of desire is increased in geometrical progression". Maybe it is true that no lasting happiness lies in the senses, but there is a lot to be said for the tastes and sounds of living, provided we can avoid clinging to them. To Ramakrishna, everyone seemed to him to be seeking glass beads, and to be rejecting diamonds, and he said that man was enamoured of lust and was caught in the glamour of wealth and riches. To one, however, who has seen God, these appear as worthless trifles.

But to one who has *not* seen God? For him, glamour retains its magic, and so long as bondage continues, there must be visions. It will be remembered that the captives in Plato's Cave could not tear themselves away from the shadows playing on the wall, but once they *saw* the light beckoning from outside the Cave, the spell was broken, and they were able to advance towards freedom. In Vivekananda's phrase, "the abracadabras fall off of themselves", and with the attainment of a higher vision, the lower vision vanishes.

After the Swami's death, various papers came to light, among them the outlines of three chapters for a book called *The Message of Divine Wisdom.* These three chapters were concerned with bondage, the Law, the Absolute and the attainment of freedom. Of the first, Vivekananda wrote, "Desire is infinite, its fulfilment limited. Desire is unlimited in everyone; the power of fulfilment varies. Thus some are more successful than others in life." The argument is carried through point by point: we desire only the pleasurable, and not the painful, vainly hoping to have the one without the other. Anyway what is desirable today has no appeal tomorrow. "We achieve success, and we are overthrown by failure; we pursue pleasure and we are pursued by pain." Whether we like it or not, the pressure is to keep moving, because the crowd insists that we never pause for thought: we cannot stop the world, however much we may want to get off. At times one is reminded of Tolstoy (who incidentally read and enjoyed Vivekananda's *Raja-Yoga*), "Our pessimism is a dread reality, our optimism is a faint cheering, making the best of a bad job."

However, aphorisms are not much consolation, and it will be useful, I think, to consider certain aspects of bondage in more detail under separate heads. For the moment, I hope at least it has been established that lifetime after lifetime has been dissipated in a wild goose chase in search of happiness; yet, time and again, we have been disappointed, because we have searched in the wrong place. In the end, the whole forest of desires will have to be ruthlessly felled, but before the axe is laid to the root, it is as well to know the nature of the tree, particularly that famous tree in the Garden of Eden.

Chapter Eleven

PASSION'S SLAVE

"What sex sows, death reaps." (Kathleen Raine)

I am always on my guard when anyone holds forth about sex; the suspicion lurks that such vociferation stems from either too much or too little experience. Admittedly, I shall be following Vivekananda in my thinking in this chapter, and I am sure that he is fundamentally right, but the awareness remains that there is no more treacherous subject upon which to dilate than that of sex. My aim will be to steer between the Scylla of disapproval and the Charybdis of permissiveness: the two extremes are epitomised in our own day by Malcolm Muggeridge and Alex Comfort. For Muggeridge, the body is seen as a "carcase", hideously tormented by dark desires: for Comfort, there can be no healthier exercise than going to bed with a "deliciously lewd" partner. Somehow neither approach really takes into account the ambivalences and ambiguities of human sexuality.

There is a notion that we are now "emancipated" as far as sex is concerned, but if Mrs. Grundy was a killjoy, it remains extremely doubtful whether modern indulgence has "solved" people's sexual hopes and fears. The trouble with even the most protracted orgasm is that it comes to an end.

Vivekananda greatly modified his views on sex in the course of his life; but the basic assumptions were constant all the way through. We have seen that in boyhood he forsook Sita and Rama in favour of Shiva, and this because the former were married. As a young man, he was determined to avoid marriage at any price; deep in him was the knowledge that his destiny demanded continence. In the course of his wanderings, he came across some Tibetans who practised polyandry, and his first reaction was one of shocked disgust at the idea of one woman being shared by several men in this way. Yet, after talking with these people, he came to see that their behaviour stemmed more from a lack of possessiveness than anything else, and he condemned himself for his earlier priggishness.

Another extraordinary experience which befell Vivekananda in India, was the time when he met up with a sect of sex-worshippers, who had in mind to force him to take part in their rites, in order to acquire certain psychic powers. They knew that this sannyasin, who had providentially come their way, had been celibate for many years, and would therefore be full of latent energies which they could tap. Fortunately the Swami managed to escape unscathed.

I mention this incident because it brings out the significant point that chastity is a way of conserving energy. It is fashionable to deride the idea of sublimation and to assume that chastity is no more than a failure to integrate one's sexuality. In his *Raja-Yoga*, Vivekananda explained how sexual energy can be converted into ojas which may be defined as virility, and is regarded by the yogis as the highest form of energy, which can be stored in the brain. The greater this store, the greater a man's power, intellectually and spiritually. All the forces working in the body become ojas in their highest form, and by the exercise of restraint, a man can transmute the base metal of lust into the gold coin of creativity.

Mention of the word "lust" must make us beware of thinking that all sexual activity is necessarily lustful, and that we should all be providently storing up ojas, instead of raising families. Not so. As Vivekananda had found with his Tibetans, there is such a thing as innocence in sex, and the old adage holds good, that to the pure, all things are pure. He wrote to an American lady in 1896 that "we have only to grasp the idea of *gradation of morality* and everything becomes clear . . ." (author's italics). And in another place he differentiates between vice and virtue by saying that the proper use of any of the faculties of mind or body is virtuous, while improper application or waste is vicious.

Vivekananda's early prejudice against marriage gave way to the realisation that for 99% of the human race, marriage is the truest goal. He heard the story of an old couple who were separated at the workhouse after half a century together as man and wife: at the end of the first day, the old man said, "Can't I see Mary and kiss her before she goes to sleep? Why, I haven't missed doing that at night for fifty years." Vivekananda exclaimed, "Marriage itself had been the path for those two souls!"

But if marriage is to be the path, it must be taken seriously, and purity is no less incumbent on the householder than on the renunciate. Few see sex's function as entirely procreative; yet there would seem to be good sense in abstinence, once the children have been born, and the family established. It entirely depends on what is desired. If the aim be pleasure, then contraceptives and other methods of birth-control are to be welcomed. If, on the other hand, a married couple wish to adventure together into the spirit, they may find, to their surprise and delight, that abstinence makes the heart grow fonder.

Vivekenanda contended that unchaste imagination is as bad as unchaste actions. In other words, mere physical celibacy is of no value whatsoever unless the mind, too, is scoured of prurience. His advice was to control desire, rather than muzzle it, "Transform the sexual energy into spiritual energy, but do not emasculate, because that is throwing away the power. The stronger this force, the more can be done with it."

If we envisage sex as a mighty river plunging and roaring towards the sea, the power can only be harnessed by damming the flood, and restricting the water to a narrow and intense flow. In this way, cities can be lit and machinery driven. It is a matter of whether we are prepared to sacrifice the savage splendour of an unbridled torrent, for the practical value of hydro-electric power. Similarly, the simple savage can drink his fill of the wine of sex, and spend his days and nights in blissful sensualism— that is his privilege as a savage. But we are not savages, and can no longer sport with Amaryllis in the shade in good conscience. There really is no basis for comparing the naive joys of primitives with the knowing pleasures of sophisticates. For the savage, fertility and fruitfulness are highly esteemed qualities, whereas in our civilization, we pride ourselves on our capacity for "enjoying sex" without having to bear the consequences. I believe that we are paying a far higher price for this in terms of spiritual impoverishment, than is usually acknowledged. Vivekananda claimed that spiritual giants are produced only where the vow of chastity is observed, and he pointed to the great saints of the Catholic Church such as St. Francis, St. Teresa, the two Catherines and so on, as evidence of this. The Protestants, on the other hand, have not produced anyone of equal stature, having no tradition of chastity.

Ramakrishna's dictum was that twelve years' continence enables a man to become open to the knowledge of God. In the case of his greatest disciple, the evidence suggests that this was literally true. Vivekananda's astonishing impact on the West, his prodigious memory, the sheer force of his presence: all bear witness to a man who knew how to conserve his energies, and then release them in the most creative possible way.

Far be it from me to suggest that sex is somehow reprehensible and the sooner we all turn celibate, the better. But perhaps we should ponder before expending our vital energies on a pleasure, which however excruciating and exquisite, is not only notoriously evanescent, but far more depleting than modern medicine has begun to appreciate.

Some readers may well feel that Vivekananda's ideas about sex are now out-of-date, and that the very idea of marriage, let alone celibate marriage, is increasingly a thing of the past. *Brave New World* is already with us, and no young person in his senses is going to let an opportunity for erotic adventure pass by. After all, did not Lawrence himself announce that the sovereign way to God lay in sexual intercourse? and more recently, Tantric Yoga has been all the rage. To which I can only say, let him who is without lust, adopt the first *asana*.

To anticipate one other probable objection to the idea of sexual restraint, it is important to distinguish between repression and suppression. Vivekananda favoured the latter, which means consciously renouncing the pleasures and pains of sex for spiritual ends. To repress, on the other hand, is to believe that an appetite doesn't exist in oneself, and that its existence in others is disgusting. Better by far to be an honest libertine, than to choke with virtue, as sex goes rancid in the subconscious.

"Give me that man that is not passion's slave!" cried Hamlet. Vivekananda was such a man, and if it's mastery we are after, then slavery must be abolished forthwith. Bondage of the sado-masochistic kind, as students of the perverse well know, has its appeal, and is not easily rejected. There is no need to dwell on the pathetic pleasures of those who like being tied up and abused, but even the most "adjusted" amongst us find it hard to cut the silken threads of sensuality and abandon the musky ardours of eroticism. If this renunciation simply amounts to giving up a good thing, then there is nothing to recommend it. Vivekananda believed and taught, however, that by renouncing sex, it is possible to gain access to far, far better things. Nevertheless, we shouldn't take his word for it: we must find out for ourselves.

Chapter Twelve

OF NO EARTHLY USE

"Mystery-mongering weakens the human brain." (Vivekananda)

In my late teens, I attended a spiritualist meeting which was being held in the local town hall. The audience consisted largely of elderly ladies, and before the maestro came on, there was a tremulous atmosphere of twittering anticipation. To my disappointment, when the show started, the lights remained undimmed, and the gentleman in rimless glasses on the stage bore no resemblance to Svengali. He pointed to various members of the audience and told them that their relatives were settling in nicely on the Other Side and generally making themselves at home there. In one instance, he reported that a deceased lady had been reunited with her parrot; in another, that someone had acquired a fine new head of hair. I left the town hall with all my prejudices about this kind of thing hideously confirmed.

Later I visited a medium in a London suburb and a Middle Eastern sage "came through" to tell me various things about myself and those close to me. I was very impressed: what was said was neither sentimental nor improbable, and events have followed the pattern outlined by my informant. I recall asking how it was possible for a discarnate entity to see into the future, and was told that for such beings, time is not what it seems to us. There was much else besides, but all I wish to emphasise is that the experience could not be dismissed as either absurd or sinister. It was curiously matter-of-fact; and yet, at the same time, I should not seek out such "guidance" again. One has to learn to be one's own guide.

Quite different in character was a recent encounter with a professional hypnotist, who used his undoubted psychic abilities in a vulgar and objectionable way. His demonstration of ESP was acceptable enough, when he told people their telephone numbers and the like. But later, he put various people into a trance and made them behave in a ridiculous and demeaning way. The whole performance left a nasty taste in my mouth.

I quote these personal experiences simply to indicate that, for me, there can be no doubt that extraordinary occurrences, which can loosely be labelled as "occult", take place from time to time. The amount of importance which we should attach to them is another matter. One of the most celebrated cases of a man who had such experiences, and later repudiated them, is that of Krishnamurti. Mary Lutyens' recent book, *Krishnamurti—the Years of Awakening*, gives a marvellous picture of the darling of the Theosophical Society. It seems that as a small boy, Krishnamurti used to have visions of Krishna, playing his flute, as traditionally depicted in Hindu art, and he attributed this experience to the fact that his mother was a devotee of Krishna. Later, when he was taken under Bishop Leadbeater's astral wing, he began to see the Master Koot Hoomi, and in the fulness of time, the Lord Maitreya appeared to him, and after that, the Buddha. In 1927, Krishnamurti answered the question, "Who brings the truth?" by saying that Krishna, Koot Hoomi, and the rest are all forms of the One Beloved, and yet reality lies beyond these forms. Two years later, Krishnamurti dissolved the Order of the Star, unequivocally rejected theosophy and all its works, and bade all who listened to him to be free from all fears, and discover with him that Truth is a pathless land. Annie Besant, Krishnamurti's protectress and spiritual mother, was heartbroken at this reverse, and contended that it was her business to go on providing crutches for the weak, who could not bear to give up their belief in the theosophical pantheon.

Actually, to say, as I have, that Krishnamurti *repudiated* his occult experiences, is rather misleading; it was simply that he came eventually to believe that ultimate truth cannot be presented fully in any one guise. He also took the line that

103

psychic powers are liable to make people over-credulous about what they have seen or heard.

Pantanjali in his famous *Aphorisms of Yoga* lists the psychic powers which yogis can attain. According to him, they can understand all languages, read others' minds, become invisible at will, change in size, create anything they like to dream up, etc. But then comes the catch, "These powers of knowledge," he says, "are obstacles to illumination; but illumination apart, they bring success".

Vivekananda made it his business to investigate such phenomena, and he witnessed remarkable accomplishments by fakirs in India, such as producing fruit and flowers out of mid-air. He was sure that man's mind contains limitless powers, which for most of us, remain dormant. So-called "miracles" need not be attributed to a supernatural being, but each individual can rather be seen as a channel for infinite knowledge and power. The knack, of course, lies in unblocking the channel, and the practice of Raja-Yoga is designed to open us to such powers. The danger is that when someone discovers that he can perform miracles, he is spiritually greatly at risk. Nothing can be more blinding to the aspirant than the realization that he has developed "special" abilities—filled with spiritual pride, he is all too liable to be corrupted by his new-found powers.

Vivekananda stressed the importance of storing up powers as they are acquired, and resisting the temptation to use them. The secret is never to *seek* powers, but to *attain* them by purity. The highly spiritual will automatically be able to do the kinds of things mentioned by Patanjali, but as to whether they will *choose* to do so, is another matter altogether. We have already seen that Vivekananda had a perfect memory of his past lives, that he was prompted by "voices" in the preparation of his lectures; it is also recorded that he could see at a distance, and that on occasion, he could pick up what people were thinking; but he never considered these powers to be marks of spirituality, and never exercised them if he could help it. Like the yogi who had a river to cross, he disdained to walk on water, but chose rather to reach the other side by way of a bridge.

Mention has already been made of theosophy: Vivekananda had scant regard for this religion and regarded it as a hotch-potch of half-understood notions which Westerners had gathered piecemeal in the East. He viewed their missionary endeavours in India with profound distaste. "We Hindus have no need nor desire to import religion from the West. Sufficient has been the degradation of importing almost everything else."

Once, when a disciple spoke of the spirit-world, and was unwise enough to read out an extract from a theosophical book, Vivekananda came down on him like a ton weight, and, in the words of an observer, "extinguished him completely". The same observer adds, "I saw that the Swami was a hater of spookism. He clearly said that all this was weakening and debilitating and had nothing to do with true religion."

As for astrology, Vivekananda dismissed it, together with "all these mystical things", as generally being signs of a weak mind and advised anyone who found himself becoming unduly obsessed by such ideas, to see a doctor at once, eat well, and have plenty of sleep. On the whole, he condemned chasing after psychic experience as a terrible waste of energy, and valued common sense and practical wisdom far more highly than the maunderings of dabblers in the occult.

In the States, of course, the Swami frequently came across people who held séances and contacted spirit "guides" of one kind and another. At one séance which he attended (Vivekananda always had to see for himself—he was never content with hearsay), the entity which had been conjured up, informed the rapt group that there was an Indian gentleman present, sitting on a bench. Vivekananda found this laughable, and as for all the attempts to "prove" life after death: to the Swami this was not only ridiculous but pathetic—for him, death was no more than a threshold, and he could not see much value in bolstering oneself up by communing with ghosts.

One of the recurring difficulties which Vivekananda had to

contend with in America, was the expectation that he would work wonders wherever he went. "Will Kananda do something handsome while in Detroit?" asked a columnist with some asperity, "Will he do nothing but talk?" In point of fact, Vivekananda's lectures *did* have unlooked-for results: people in the audience used sometimes to get into an ecstatic state, but afterwards, by way of reaction, they would experience "an excess of the carnal instinct". The Swami's aim, of course, was not to work people up into a state of high emotion; nor yet did he want to display or impart amazing abilities. If some of his listeners were temporarily thrown off balance by his presence, he attributed this to their lack of steady practice in meditation and concentration. Vivekananda's constant concern was to strengthen and encourage, and, as he saw it, any excursions into the weird and wonderful, could only weaken and discourage in the long run.

The Swami once spoke about the basis for psychical research and made the crucial point that in order to have a scientific explanation of a psychic phenomenon, not only is perfect evidence required, but also "a good deal of training on the part of those who want to see". We all know the cautionary tale of the sorcerer's apprentice: he who meddles with magic before he knows enough about it, is apt to find things getting out of hand.

We need not share Hotspur's scepticism, when Glendower declared that he could "call spirits from the vasty deep". So can we, if we will. Again, it is no whimsy to believe with Longfellow that "the spirit world around this world of sense, floats like an atmosphere". I am persuaded, for example, that F. W. H. Myers (author of *Human Personality and its Survival of Bodily Death*) was a man of integrity both in life, and in death, and that he was able to communicate his safe arrival in the hereafter to his surviving friends, as he had promised he would. For Vivekananda, however, all this was really by the way. It is true that after death, people experience whatever they are ready for: for some, this means "Heaven", for others, "Hell". But neither state lasts forever, and both are merely aspects of maya in another dimension. As Vivekananda succinctly put it, " the wicked see this universe as hell, and the partially good see it as heaven, while perfect beings realize it as God Himself". Be they alive or be they dead, they bind their souls to make their bed.

When Ramakrishna offered to transfer all his supernatural powers to Naren (as he then was), the young man asked, "Will they help me to realize God?" "No," said the Master, "but they will be useful to you *after* realization."

Naren was content to wait.

We must wait too, and not allow ourselves to be drawn into the beguiling realm of the occult. None can deny the fascination and excitement of the uncanny and the strange, but not only is it of no earthly use, but it's of no spiritual use either. This is not to close our minds to phenomena such as ESP or astral travel, but to realize that, at best, they are by-products of the good life, and if pursued as ends in themselves, can only end in confusion and disaster. Look, for instance, at what happened to Aleister Crowley: a young man of enormous promise and tremendous gifts who gradually became more and more drawn to evil so that now his name is synonymous with the grotesque and the ugly. In the photographs which appear in his "autohagiography", one can see an appalling degeneration setting in, as he got increasingly fascinated by the powers which came to him as a magician. Not only did he become evil, but he became silly as well; it seems to be a mark of those who go in for magic, that they get so puffed up with their self-importance, that they lose touch with reality, and make fools of themselves.

Our aim must be for timeless Reality, not for psychic gifts which are tied to time and space. Once it has clearly been understood that psychic and spiritual powers are quite different in kind, then more than half the battle is won. But there can be no doubt that there is a tremendous pull exerted by the occult: a glance at magazines which deal with witchcraft shows that there is a close link between the desire for magical powers, and the craving for sexual adventure. I recall C. S. Lewis writing of the lust which is felt as a salty tang in the throat, and this is when one is drawn towards what have been well named the powers of darkness. Young people in particular seem to go through a phase of table-turning, meeting in graveyards, lighting black candles and so on. Up to a point, it is pretty harmless, but I have seen enough of what *can* happen, to agree with Vivekananda that mystery-mongering weakens the human brain. Probably the worst of psychic high jinks is that they get you nowhere from the spiritual point of view, and they may well have an adverse effect when people become obsessed by the bizarre experiences which come their way. One must be prepared to give up that kind of excitement, if the goal is freedom; of all kinds of bondage, the psychic variety is the most insidious because it gives an illusion of power.

It is only by being breathtakingly humble that one can attain to that power and glory which Jesus spoke of: all else is arrogance and must end in nemesis.

Chapter Thirteen

DISAPPEARANCES

"My son, there is nothing in this world that is not God." (Mundaka Upanishad)

Eli, the High Priest, waited in the gateway at Shiloh—old, blind and forlorn. He was waiting for news of what promised to be a decisive battle between the Philistines and the Israelites in the hill-country at Aphek. A messenger dashed breathlessly up to him covered with sweat, his clothes in tatters to signify mourning: the Israelites had been defeated and 30,000 soldiers lay dead on the battlefield, including the High Priest's own two sons. But worse was to come: the Ark of the Covenant had been taken. This last was too much for the old man, and he fell over backwards from his seat by the side of the gate, and broke his neck.

One of Eli's sons, Phinehas, left a widow who was expecting a child. When she learnt of what had happened, the shock caused her to go into labour immediately, and she only lived long enough to indicate what she wished her son to be called. The Book of Samuel records that she named the child Ichabod, saying the glory had departed from Israel because of the disastrous consequences of the Philistine victory.

The Ark of the Covenant was inestimably precious to the Jews, and the Philistines knew that by capturing it they had played a master stroke. The Ark embodied the spirit of the Jewish race, the Spirit of their God, and with its loss, the glory had indeed departed from Israel. "Ichabod" in Hebrew means "inglorious", and this explains the dying woman's choice of name—in the absence of God, there can be no glory.

I have begun this chapter with the story of Ichabod because his name so exactly conveys the idea of maya. The "Ichabod Effect" may be defined as the human tendency to be taken in by appearances, until such time as reality declares itself.

It is consoling to know that Vivekananda sweated over trying to explain the nature of maya. To describe maya as illusion is apt to make one think of God as a kind of Cosmic Wizard, who delights in bemusing his creatures with sleight of the Divine Hand. Indeed, the Upanishads suggest that "as a magician He appears in many forms". Another synonym for maya is enchantment, which carries with it the idea of having been cast under a spell. Maya has also been likened to a cloud of ignorance, to a distorting lens through which we view reality, to "a parable in action". This last phrase is a useful one, and I am indebted to Aldous Huxley for it. He suggested that while the phenomenon is symbolical, and not ultimately real, it remains a parable in action.

On March 25, 1896, the Swami delivered a lecture before the Graduate Philosophical Society of Harvard University, and in that lecture he sought to explain the difference between what *seems* and what *is*. He gave the well-known example of the snake and the rope: a man sees what he at first takes to be a snake, and backs away in alarm—however, once he has plucked up the courage to make a closer investigation, he discovers that he was mistaken, and that he had allowed himself to be frightened by a mere piece of rope. Hence, the snake was the *phenomenon*, whereas the rope is the *noumenon*. There has been no change, except in the observer.

The same principle applies to our appreciation and apprehension of the universe as a whole. When one is in ignorance (under a misapprehension, if you like), then only the phenomena can be detected, and God is invisible. However, once God stands revealed, the universe simply disappears, and "there is nothing in this world which is not God". Both Ramakrishna and Vivekananda experienced this at Dakshineswar when "houses, doors, temples and everything else vanished altogether".

To return to Huxley's "parable in action", we can say therefore that our experiences in the sphere of time, space and causation, are immensely useful to us, because they give us a framework in which to learn, and to grow towards a recognition of our real identity. But all these experiences are phenomena; or in more poetic language, thoughts in the Mind of God. Instead of brute facts, we must come to discern the allegorical and symbolical meaning *behind* appearances. When Jesus told the parable of the Prodigal Son, he was saying that we are all wayward sons and daughters, who will eventually see the folly of starving to death in a far country, come to ourselves, and set out for home.

Vivekananda was often asked how the Absolute can become relative and he replied that this is not a meaningful question. God is only *apparently* the material cause of the universe: in reality, the cause is the effect in another form. We conceive of a separation between Creator and created, but this is because our minds are geared to dualistic thinking. Like men in the desert, we imagine we can see water and palm trees, whereas in fact, there is nothing there—it is a mirage. However, if we realize that it *is* a mirage and that it comes and goes; we shall continue to see it, but with this difference—that it will no longer deceive us. Hence, when a man has realized his own nature, "the whole world has vanished for him. It will come back again, but no more the same world of misery".

For myself, I find with each succeeding year, that the solidity and reliability of the material world grows less and less real to me. The tangible certainties of childhood and youth have given way to a burgeoning cloud of unknowing. The *Brihadaranyaka Upanishad* speaks of "disappearances", "Father disappears, mother disappears, world disappears, gods disappear . . ." It isn't that they've gone, but rather that one sees them in a new light, which strips them of what one formerly took to be their nature.

If the world only exists in relation to a mind, then it has no real existence, and yet it nonetheless exists. So ran Vivekananda's argument. This is reminiscent of the famous analogy of the gramophone playing to itself in the wilderness:

unless there is an ear to hear, there is no sound, and yet there is vibration. In his lecture on *Maya and Illusion*, the Swami spoke of the manifold appearance of maya, and he suggested some of its more distressing effects. We cling to life and we cannot give it up: this is maya. We are after the Golden Fleece and we think we shall never die: this is maya. We yearn to be happy, and find that we are miserable: this is maya. In a subsequent lecture he put forward the idea that "as we grow, so the gods grow", and indeed, if we trace the development of man's religious beliefs, we shall see the truth of this. The Vikings conceived of gods in their own image—bluff, tough characters, who liked nothing better than risking their necks in an endless search for adventure. Think of Thor, the eternal boy, off to the Land of the Giants, armed with his mighty hammer and capable of tremendous feats of strength and endurance. The Red Indians imagined a future life in the shape of a Happy Hunting Ground, fat with buffalo, all ready for sharp-eyed braves with their swift arrows. Calvinists, at least of the stricter kind, have found consolation in the doctrine that all those who differ from them, will languish for all eternity in a kind of super-Auschwitz. Such notions give way to the idea of God Almighty, the All-Good, and the Ever-Merciful, Who is in charge of the entire universe. But of course such a God does not account for the existence of evil and it is therefore necessary to have his opposite number, the Devil. All these pictures of Reality are befogged by the haze of maya until at last, the pilgrim emerges into the clear white light of the Impersonal Absolute, and realizes that All is One.

An infallible sign that maya is starting to lose its magic, is when a seeker after truth begins to appreciate with full force the terrible futility of human endeavour. No matter how hard we may strive to achieve our ends, ultimately death and decay reduce everything to dust and ashes. "We cannot hide a carrion with roses . . ." declared Vivekananda in characteristically vivid metaphor, "so with our lives. We may try to cover our old and festering sores with a cloth of gold; but there comes a day when the cloth of gold is removed, and the sore in all its ugliness is revealed."

The time must come when we tire of the way of the world, and cannot rest easy until we have found another way, which genuinely satisfies our deepest longings. We are no longer content "to put up with" life, but are determined to live in very truth. Once this determination has really established itself, then what used to look so daunting, or so pointless, suddenly acquires a quite new character, and the former prison-house is miraculously transformed into a playground. This is what Vivekananda called the "deification" of life, when the insubstantiality of the world becomes evident and we no longer cry out for glass beads, but insist on diamonds. Blessed are they who "having nothing, yet possessing all things", no longer pine for fulfilment and satisfaction in the miasma of maya, but recognize that their destiny calls them relentlessly to eternity. They have seen that "as threads come from the spider, as little sparks come from the fire, so all senses, all conditions, all gods, all beings come from the Self". *(Brihadaranyaka Upanishad)*

Over and again, Vivekananda says that we suffer from hallucinations and delusions and are so taken up with the names and forms of the many, that the One passes us by. A thousand impressions bombard us every hour; people come and people go; events flash by, and God is eclipsed by swarms of imbecilities. We evade what Gerald Heard called "the appalling instaneity of God", partly because it is simply too much for us, but mainly because our attention is held by other things. We are dying of thirst, and our desperate search for the water of life takes us anywhere and everywhere but to the river which flows at our feet. Like the king who went mad, we look for His Majesty; like crazed explorers, we seek an empire which has never been lost.

Strictly speaking, it cannot be said that the soul evolves: it has always been perfect, and always will be. The very notion of imperfection is the product of maya, and it would be more true to refer to original virtue than to original sin. In an admirably lucid letter to E. T. Sturdy written from New York in 1896,

Vivekananda explained how the soul *appears* to go through various stages. The first of these stages is in the solar sphere of visible universe, when the soul's identity is obscured by the mask of a physical body. Next comes the lunar sphere or the habitation of the gods, which is the experience of those whose good karma has earned them a spell of astral bliss. Later stages enable the soul to contemplate the entire universe, until in the end, knower and known are no longer separate and the soul becomes aware of its unity with God: it neither came nor went through all these successive stages, but "as it was in the beginning, is now and ever shall be, world without end, amen".

What we experience is what we are fitted to experience, and our conception of heaven changes with the change of our necessities. We pass through all the teeming variety of life, and each time what at first looked like a real landscape, turns out to be painted scenery. It's easy to see why man's experience has so often been likened to that of an actor who "struts and frets his hour upon the stage". Shakespeare was right to describe life as "but a walking shadow"; but it does not follow from this that "it is a tale told by an idiot, full of sound and fury, signifying nothing". It signifies both everything and nothing. We play many different parts in the drama, some good, some bad, and Vivekananda was certain that when the dream is finished, and we have left the stage, we shall have a hearty laugh at all we have undergone.

The secret of successful acting is to be able to play a part convincingly without becoming emotionally involved. The difference between a professional and an amateur actor lies precisely in this. The amateur puts everything into the performance, and at the end of it, he is spent: the professional, on the other hand, stays detached, even when the exigencies of his role demand suffering or death. He remains the witness of his adopted persona, and as a result, is able to play his part to the best advantage.

Vivekananda made some very paradoxical statements about maya; that it is real in that the Real is behind it and gives it its

114

appearance of reality; that he who knows the Real sees in maya not illusion, but reality; that he who does *not* know the Real sees in maya illusion and thinks it real. I leave the reader to sort all that out for himself! Less baffling was his assurance that every moment we are actually enjoying absolute bliss, "though covered up, misunderstood, and caricatured". In order to understand that, there is no alternative but to, "give up ignorance, and all that is false, and then truth will begin to reveal itself to us". To vary the proverb: if wisdom is bliss, 'tis folly to be ignorant, which, for all its metrical inelegance, effectively sums the matter up.

The enormous attraction of ignorance is that it leaves us free to make our own mistakes, and most of the time the attraction is irresistible: that is why we fall victim to the "Ichabod Effect" and the glory departs with depressing regularity with each new disillusionment. Sooner or later, the "disappearances" begin to multiply at an ever-increasing rate: fathers, mothers, worlds and gods are joined by thieves, monks, masters and servants, until finally with the disappearance of good and evil, we find we have gone beyond sorrow into the land of the free. Or as Vivekananda put it, "The moment I have realized God sitting in the temple of every human body, the moment I stand in reverence before every human being and see God in him—that moment I am free from bondage, everything that binds, vanishes, and I am free."

Chapter Fourteen

THE EASY YOKE

"Without charity the mere outward work profiteth nothing: but whatsoever is done of charity, be it never so little and contemptible in the sight of the world, becomes wholly fruitful. For God weigheth more with how much love a man worketh than how much he doeth. He doeth much that loveth much." (Thomas à Kempis)

Vivekananda always maintained that the only way out of maya is right through the thick of it, and there can never be any justification for sinking into a listless torpor in which life just "happens" to one. Fatalism of this kind prevailed for centuries in the East, and the Swami never tired of castigating his countrymen for their failure to come to grips with the demands of modern life. In order to see the need for hard work, the idea of karma has to be taken to heart. Like maya, karma is frequently used as an excuse for laziness. Nowadays, with the rise in knowledge of matters esoteric, there is a tendency to answer all problems with the remark, "Oh well, it's karma, you know." Which is not to realize that karma is made to be broken.

Little sense can be made of karma, unless the nature of samskaras (or sanskaras) is firmly grasped. A samskara is an inherent tendency in a living organism towards a particular kind of behaviour. For the present purpose, we shall confine our attention to human beings, but the principle applies at all levels of manifestation. Samskaras can be good or bad, ancient or modern, slight or pronounced—but some are basic to all of us, and will come to the surface, given the right conditions.

At first glance, I may believe myself to be a twentieth edition of homo sapiens; tolerably educated, apparently civilized, cast in a Western European middle-class mould. However, below this thin veneer of acquired characteristics, there is much that I may find it expedient to hide, if I wish to pass muster as a good fellow. It makes little difference whether one thinks in terms of reincarnation or a collective unconscious: either way, there are traces, more or less palpable, of a past which includes animal instincts, brutish appetites, and primitive desires. Take away my food and drink for a little while, and I shall probably revert to far from bland behaviour. Put me to the torture, and elemental fears will bubble to the surface. In other words, my present face is a cover for earlier, more uncouth selves, and I carry the samskaras in my bloodstream, as it were.

Sometimes in situations where inhibitions have been released, it is all too easy to lose sight of a person's humanity, as the bull or the bear or the pig takes over. The story of Circe, the enchantress, who turned Ulysses' companions into beasts, contains an allegorical truth which is germane here. Samskaras common to all, are those persistent natural desires which mere conditioning can never entirely destroy. If I am greedy, lustful, selfish, or violent, that is because of my inherited samskaras— the old man yet lives.

Fortunately, the situation is not as bleak as might be supposed. If human beings were entirely at the mercy of samskaras of this kind, no one would be able to withstand the call of the wild. The observable facts do not tally with this. For example, in the Nazi extermination camps, many prisoners degenerated into whimpering animals, it is true; but not all, not by any means all. So the question arises, "Why are some so much better fitted for adversity than others?"

Samskaras are not really thrust upon us: we are creating them incessantly. Every thought, word and deed, makes its mark on the matrix of the mind and the resultant recording is completely faithful to what has passed. What I am now, rests wholly on what I have been; and what I shall be, depends entirely on what I am. Supposing, let us say, that many lifetimes ago, I was faced with a challenge, and that I failed to measure up to it. Inevitably that challenge must recur over and over again, till I am able to overcome my fear in order to meet it. This doesn't mean that the same situation recurs, but a similar one, and the test is repeated until I have passed it, and am therefore in a position to go on to the next stage. If I have succeeded in resisting a temptation in the past, then I shall be the more able to resist any future temptations of the same kind—in fact, they will cease to be remotely tempting. It is in this way, that the so-called "good" samskaras are made.

If samskaras are *latent* states, vrittis are *actual* states which are plain to behold. My greed, for instance, may not be obvious until I am seen actually wolfing food, but the fact that the samskara of greed is there, means that a vritti can leap into life at the slightest provocation. That is why the samskaras have to be totally uprooted and destroyed: there can be no half-measures.

Vrittis can lead either towards bondage and suffering, or towards freedom and illumination. The first stage, therefore, is to subdue the bad vrittis with the good ones, and for this purpose, ethical and spiritual disciplines are needed. In the end, the good vrittis have to go as well, for true freedom to be won. Bad vrittis are those which augment the sense of ego, and are characterized by a grasping and acquisitive approach to life. This is a centripetal process in which everything revolves towards the centre, and an individual's specific gravity may be said to grow ever more dense and concentrated, so that he becomes locked within himself. Good vrittis, on the other hand, are actions which can broadly be described as moral and religious, and constitute a centrifugal process away from the centre, which spirals out into infinity.

In daily experience we veer between good and bad vrittis, between expansion and contraction; nevertheless, each lifetime carries one a little further in one direction or the other. The miser, for example, is so obsessed with amassing wealth, that he ends his days in a frenzy of precaution, lest he lose some of his money: for him, the music of the spheres has degenerated into the forlorn clink of gold on gold. The saint, by contrast, in his single-minded zeal for "that which does not pass away", reaches a stage where he is prepared to abandon himself to God

118

without any reservation whatsoever, and for him, the reward is eternal life. The miser might be said to exemplify galloping egotism, while the saint epitomizes selflessness.

Outside fiction, such extremes rarely exist, but we have all met people who have withered into selfishness; equally, some of us may have had the good fortune to encounter men and women who somehow enhance experience, both for themselves and for others. The cardinal error is to believe that the direction in which one travels is predestined. It is entirely up to us to ensure that we develop as we should. The seed is there: it is simply a matter of allowing it to germinate.

This is not to underrate the difficulties involved in dealing with one's karma: anyone who imagines that there is such a thing as life without tears is doomed to disappointment. We should think rather in Churchillian terms of blood and sweat, and then there may be some chance of victory. The curious thing is, though, that once the worst has been faced the challenge turns out to be much less daunting than was imagined.

Vivekananda defined the tremendous force which is called "character" as the sum total of samskaras. This character has been created over many lifetimes and the balance of good and bad samskaras at the time of death determines the direction a person will take in his next life. "A man dies," said the Swami, "the body falls away and goes back to the elements, but the samskaras remain, adhering to the mind which, being made of finer material, does not dissolve, because the finer the material, the more persistent it is. But the mind dissolves in the long run, and that is what we are struggling for."

This chapter, and the three following it, will be concerned with the four Yogas which Vivekananda did so much to clarify and explain. The four are: Karma-Yoga, or the yoga of work; Bhakti-Yoga, or the yoga of love; Raja-Yoga or the yoga of mind control; and Jnana-Yoga or the yoga of knowledge. Temperament and other factors predispose one towards one of these four, but it should be emphasized at the outset, that, most

119

commonly, individuals find that their path will lead them through all the different kinds of yoga, and there are no hard and fast distinctions.

The basis for Karma-Yoga is to be found in the *Bhagavad-Gita*, and since Vivekananda scarcely ever gave a lecture without quoting from the *Gita*, a brief look at that great spiritual poem will not come amiss.

In the introduction to his excellent translation of the *Gita*, Juan Mascaró writes that it is the story of the battle between the light and the dark, and the temptation to withdraw from the battle. Arjuna becomes the soul of man, and Krishna, the charioteer of the soul. As the *Gita*'s message is essentially spiritual, details such as when precisely it was written, or by whom, need not detain us, and there is no call therefore to indulge in what Vivekananda used to call "text-torturing".

At the beginning of the poem, Arjuna is in a state of confusion and dismay, faced as he is with the prospect of doing battle with his kinsmen. Krishna tells him that death is not to be feared, and besides, a man is duty bound to fight in a just war, provided, of course, that he has no thought of personal gain. Arjuna is not entirely reassured by this, so that Krishna reiterates the importance of doing what has to be done, simply and solely for the sake of doing it. "He whose undertakings are free from anxious desire and fanciful thought, whose work is made pure in the fire of wisdom: he is called wise by those who see."

Arjuna then protests that this is all very well, but he is at odds with himself, and his mind is restless. To which Krishna replies peremptorily, "What of the restless mind? It *can* be pacified, given hard work."

As the *Gita* unfolds, Krishna emerges as "the One source of all", and, at one point, nearly terrifies Arjuna out of his wits by revealing his full splendour and radiance, so that the whole universe in its variety is seen as "standing in a vast unity in the body of the God of gods". Such a revelation cannot be borne by those enslaved by the deadly trinity of lust, anger and greed, and the task is therefore to renounce all selfish works and to surrender the reward of all work to God.

Man is subject to three qualities or tendencies, which are described in the *Gita* as the three gunas of sattva, rajas, and tamas. Sattva corresponds with the element of air, and manifests itself in the ability to be calm and stable, and to engage in contemplation and meditation. Rajas, corresponding with fire, is that dynamic force of energy and action, which expresses itself in displays of power, and in a regal capacity for enjoyment. Tamas, corresponding with earth, is a state in which inertia and sluggishness stifle creative action, and the qualities of fire and light are quenched and dimmed.

At first, it might seem that the sattvic type is to be preferred, but the danger for him is that he can get overattached to serenity for its own sake. Again, rajasic energies are liable to run amok, and lead people to behave rashly because they crave the consolation of action. Tamas serves a useful purpose in anchoring energies, so that they don't become dissipated in airy notions or consumed in fiery passions; the tamasic guna should not therefore be summarily dismissed.

The secret of success lies in going *beyond* the three gunas, by getting them into a state of perfect balance. Such a balance has been reached by a man who is able to contemplate the heavens as he goes about his daily business, with his feet planted securely on the ground. The repeated lesson of the *Bhagavad-Gita* is that action is greater than inaction, and any attempt to evade struggle is hopeless, because sooner or later battle must be joined, and the enemy slain. Obviously the poem should not be read literally (any more than the book of *Genesis* should be taken at face value) and it will mean very little until we have seen that it is concerned with wider issues than the waverings of an obscure princeling in 500 B.C. Arjuna is Everyman, and that ancient clash of arms on the plains of India is echoed inside each one of us now, as the forces of good and evil continue to vie for supremacy.

In Chapter XV of the *Gita*, "the most secret doctrine" is

121

revealed by Krishna, "He who with a clear vision sees me as the Spirit Supreme, he knows all there is to be known, and he adores me with all his soul." Given such a vision, a man will have both the motive and the ability to work willingly and effectively in whatever capacity is required of him.

Vivekananda's Karma-Yoga lectures amount to an extended gloss on the *Gita*, and we are now in a position to explore the Swami's teachings in this field. In the introduction to the first edition of Vivekananda's *Complete Works* the editors freely confessed that the truths he preached would have been as true, had he never been born, "the difference would have lain in their difficulty of access, in their want of modern clearness and incisiveness of statement, and in their loss of mutual coherence and unity". Nowhere is this more true than in what Vivekananda had to say about the secret of work.

Really effective work, he affirmed, is done by men of immense will-power, and such will-power is not developed overnight. It is all a matter of focus, so that energies are directed into a laser beam which cuts through all difficulties. There is more to this than an economy of time and motion, although obviously a successful worker wastes neither time nor motion. The Swami laid great stress on the fact that motive is all-important. It is not *what* we do, but *why* we do it, which determines how it is done. "All outgoing energy following a selfish motive is frittered away", so that any hope of reward for one's work in the shape of wealth, fame or power is bound to end in disillusionment, sooner or later. This may not be as obvious as being struck down by a thunderbolt; but the leakage of energy will insidiously take place nonetheless, whether we are aware of it or not, and eventually, like Samson, we shall find our locks have been shorn while we slept.

If, conversely, a man is driven solely by the desire to work for work's sake, then all the power which he sends out will return to him, and the circuit of energy will be complete. The nature of the work matters not at all: it can be anything from painting a picture to sweeping the gutter. The mistake is to establish the value of a piece of work on the basis of its material results, so that all the kudos goes to those whose achievement is *measurably* impressive. Other activities are either taken for granted as necessary drudgery, or dismissed as "pointless". Upon examination it will be found that most work has its point, once you can see it, and Vivekananda refused to concede that any work is without merit. As for results: they can only be assessed quantitatively, and for Vivekananda, the significant evaluation was qualitative. Since we cannot possibly determine how spiritually valuable any given activity is, the results must be left to look after themselves.

What each person has to discover is just what it is that he is supposed to be doing with his life, and when an ideal has been decided upon, then every effort must be made to accomplish it. What other people think of that ideal doesn't matter, "each is great in his own place, but the duty of the one is not the duty of the other". The aim must be then to work without producing samskaras, and this can only be done by non-attached action.

Let us suppose that our task consists of driving a car from Lands End to John o' Groats. Clearly maps will have to be referred to in advance to decide on the best route, but once the journey has started, the driver has only one immediate duty—to make sure that he keeps his vehicle on the road. In the event of an accident he may never reach his destination.

No matter what the activity, Montaigne's dictum holds good, it is the journey and not the arrival that matters. The artist has to concentrate on each separate brush-stroke, the bricklayer must concern himself with one brick at a time, the farmer can only attend to the job in hand. Given the right approach to work, and provided there is no attachment to results, then, Vivekananda assures us, we shall be led "to the highest realization of the perfection of the soul".

It is very human to expect our work to be appreciated, and to feel that, without our efforts, the world will seize up. But the stark truth is, that if you or I died tomorrow, the world would carry on regardless, because we are not actually *needed* at all.

123

Work is a privilege, not a burden, in that it gives us the opportunity to realize ourselves by way of self-abnegation. The situation is not important: there is always work to be done, although sometimes it will require a little imagination to find it. The unanimous verdict of those who have really been called upon to suffer, is that in certain circumstances work actually consists of suffering without bitterness or recrimination. Too often, work is equated with paid employment, and a man "goes off to work" each day in order to earn a living. The trouble is that work, in that sense, is frequently seen as a compelling necessity, and everything done under compulsion goes to build up attachment.

For those who have evolved to a sufficient level of purity, work is not necessary at all—their thoughts are their justification. But most of us have to work out our impurities, and it is infinitely heartening to realize that each moment is another chance to further this process. So long as the idea of work as a privilege is uppermost, then there can be no attachment, and this is a privilege which can never be withdrawn, whether we are in the clamour of a big city, or the quiet of the outback. "The ideal man is he who, in the midst of the greatest silence and solitude, finds the intensest activity, and in the midst of the intensest activity finds the silence and solitude of the desert." In other words, a man who is really in control of himself, is immune to his surroundings; he can fulfil Rudyard Kipling's requirement of manhood, by keeping his head while all around are losing theirs.

Living, as we do, in an era of industrial disputes and economic malaise, the whole concept of work has been debased. Everything is made as quickly as possible by people who care little for craftsmanship, and rely on getting away with botched and inadequate work. The inventions of synthetic materials and labour-saving machinery have resulted in a uniform shoddiness of production, which is now taken for granted. We no longer expect articles to be well made, and anyone who puts his heart into his work is regarded as a fool.

Vivekananda suggested that the mark of the truly great is how they do *little* things, and this is a good yardstick for measuring the extent to which Karma-Yoga is being practised. Notice how a shop-assistant wraps up a parcel, how a carpenter handles his tools, how a nurse makes a bed. Much can be learnt about a man by observing the way in which he washes his hands, his manner of picking up a teacup, or how he places the needle on a record. I recall being urged to watch Krishnamurti cleaning his car, with the assurance that this would convey more to me of his teaching than a thousand lectures. Perhaps Pascal has summed the matter up best by saying that "the virtue of a man ought to be measured, not by his extraordinary exertions, but by his everyday conduct".

Can one conceive of a viable commercial enterprise run on Karma-Yoga lines? I think it might be possible, but it would need a far more complete harmony between labour and management than has been achieved so far. The most important requirement would be for all who worked in such an organization to have a job which suited them, and which they found interesting. When D. H. Lawrence declared that "work should be an absorbing game", he was enunciating a basic principle of Karma-Yoga, but it is difficult to see how current methods of factory production conduce to such a possibility. People like E. S. Schumacher (author of *Small is Beautiful*) took the view that the way of salvation lies in the creation of work which is small-scale and locally based, giving people the chance to find meaning and fulfilment in their working hours. This is good thinking, and there are already signs that this idea is being put into successful practice in many parts of the country.

Although Vivekananda was interested in schemes and plans of improvement, the main emphasis of his teaching was on preparing oneself for the work most perfectly adapted to one's potential. His emphasis was on means rather than ends. Our first task therefore must be to set our own house in order, and then we shall be in a position to start on whatever job is waiting for us. "Fill the brain with high thought, highest ideals, place

125

them day and night before you, and out of that will come great work." This was the Swami's advice, and there can be little doubt that those who have had most to give to humanity, have taken this counsel to wondrous effect. Critics of Karma-Yoga argue that it is all very well to talk in such lofty terms about the dignity of labour and so forth, but this does not take account of the enormous inequalities of ability and opportunity. If life is seen as a race, many of the contestants would appear to be so severely handicapped, that they will be lucky to be able to totter round the course, let alone take it at a gallop. To accept all the implications of the law of karma means an unblinkered acknowledgement of the apparently cruel disparities which exist between one person and another. What karma explains is that each individual is responsible for what he is, and he has the power to make himself whatever he wishes to be. Mozart was Mozart because he had laid hold of his genius and made it flesh: others, stupefied by limitation and shackled with impediment, must learn humbler lessons, but no one's bondage is so total as to make progress impossible.

Karma-Yoga, therefore, is not an esoteric doctrine, which requires us to withdraw to a Himalayan retreat and reject the dirty devices of the world. Quite the reverse, it is the yoga par excellence for modern man, enabling him to shake off the role of the wage-slave, and start being a worker in a different spirit altogether. Ideally, we should have been taught how to establish an inner balance and harmony as children, before entering the jungle of adult working life. Our schooling has failed most of us in that respect, but mercifully education can be a continuous process, and it is possible to develop qualities of resilience on the battlefield itself. That was what Arjuna learn from Krishna, and if we read the *Bhagavad-Gita* aright, we can learn the same lesson. Life is in itself religion, and once this has really sunk in, we shall discover that our work is cut out for us by the tailors of destiny; all inertia will fall away as if it had never been, and we shall see that Jesus was in earnest when he said that His yoke was easy. But, of course, you have to bow to the yoke first.

Chapter Fifteen

THE WAY OF LOVE

"If you can love your wife, you have all the religion in the world . . . but can you love?" (Vivekananda)

"Nobody loves me!" is a sufficiently harrowing *cri de coeur*, but real desolation begins with serious doubt as to whether I am capable of love myself. We all love after our own fashion, as best we can, but an honest self-examination will reveal that much of our apparent love for others is dictated by self-interest, by the desire to be accepted and loved in return. It is rare that our love is genuine enough to make us forget ourselves in a real concern for another's welfare. Nevertheless there *is* often a measure of self-forgetfulness, and the greater our conquest of egotism, the higher our chances of experiencing compassion. If pleasure-seekers are driven by the desire to satisfy themselves and fall victim to the law of diminishing returns: lovers, insofar as they are worthy of the name, are surprised by joy.

Vivekananda stated categorically that God is the one goal of all our passions and emotions, and this idea is also to be found in the words of the Scottish Catechism that "man's chief end is to glorify God, and to enjoy Him forever". But children don't think like that. In early life, a child's love is naturally directed towards his parents, and his conceptions of good and bad derive from the example and behaviour of his father and mother. At first, the mother is the dominant influence, but later the father takes pride of place. Gradually the child sees that his parents are not as powerful or as marvellous as he at first thought, so that adolescence tends to be a time of disenchantment when young people "reject" their parents: however, what they are rejecting is not the parents themselves, but *images* of the parents.

New idols follow the old, and teenagers are notoriously susceptible to the glamour of "stars" of various kinds, be they athletes, musicians, or actors. And, of course, there is also the shattering experience of "falling in love" which is the prime example of idealizing someone else, and attributing every possible and impossible excellence to them. Eventually the beloved remains the same beloved for long enough to make marriage plausible, and this can lead on to child-worship, as the family gets established. The craving for an ideal does not die with marriage, and it is not uncommon for husbands and wives to become embroiled in the heady excitements of "affairs" as a substitute for the emotions they formerly experienced with each other. For others, passions are more decorously channelled into an admiration for a hero or heroine, and there is the wish to be "just like" the paragon in question.

In my own case, my heroes have changed over the years to correspond with the truth of the moment. At school, I paid homage to the masters who seemed to me to be what I wanted to be—interesting, amusing and knowledgeable. As an ardent would-be pianist, I successively doted on Charlie Kunz, "Fats" Waller and Art Tatum. For a short period in my late teens, I conceived an immoderate enthusiasm for the novels of Evelyn Waugh, because he so perfectly exemplified the kind of cynicism which I then affected. Oscar Wilde and Aldous Huxley followed for similar reasons, but these writers both opened my eyes to deeper possibilities, and in the fulness of time came a passionate regard for George Orwell, an intense enthusiasm for Arthur Koestler, and a deep affection for Leonard Woolf. And then, of course, there was Vivekananda
. . .

Each ideal represented something which I wanted above all else to be, and I loved my "gods" because I aspired to their gifts. Oh, to play like a Waller, write like an Orwell, or teach like a Vivekananda!

It is not for nothing that one speaks of "gods" in this connection; all human beings have such deities and even the most rabid atheist will often be found to be devoted to someone whom he regards as a "master". To believe in God is simply to believe in *the* Master, to carry love and admiration through to its logical conclusion. But we cannot love an abstraction, and that is why, according to Ramakrishna, God "assumes any form for the pleasure of His devotee".

Bhakti is an intense love of God and a bhakta is a devotee of God: Bhakti-Yoga, then, is the path of devotion, the way of love. The object of worship varies from one religion to another, but each Master remains an aspect of the One Self. In *The Flame and the Light*, Hugh I'Anson Fausset suggests that each of the Masters reveals a different aspect of God: Krishna stands for the joy of the divine; Jesus, for the divine spirit as it suffers in the growing soul and redeems it by the sacrifice of love on the cross of existence; Buddha, for the breaking of bondage. The "real" historical figures of Jesus or Krishna matter less to the devotee than their archetypal mythical significance. "One might say," writes Fausset, "that a man is only real in the degree that he is a myth. For that is his eternal image. And that is what survives the death of the actual man."

Once, when Vivekananda was sailing back to India through the Mediterranean, he had a curious dream as the ship was passing the coast of Crete. An old, wise man appeared in the dream and said he was one of the ancient order of Theraputae, and added that "the truths and ideals preached by us have been given out by Christians as taught by Jesus; but for the matter of that, there was no such personality by the name of Jesus ever born." (History does not relate whether Vivekananda gave this dream credence or not).

It can be argued, therefore, that the existence or otherwise of an historical Jesus, does not necessarily detract from a devotee's worship of God *in the form of Jesus Christ*. Vivekananda contended that "Christ and Buddha were the names of a state to be attained; Jesus and Gautama were the persons to manifest it." He also suggested that the proof of the Buddhas and the Christs is that we feel like them, that they present us with an ideal which we intuitively sense lies within our own hearts. Being human, we are obliged to think of God as a person, and

129

part of the divine economy has been to supply us with God-Men and Men-Gods upon whom to focus our devotion. Until the Spirit is made flesh and dwells amongst us, we cannot accept it, bound as we are to a materialistic outlook: we can only understand the precept through the example. Vivekananda regretted the necessity for such examples, "would to God that all of us were so developed that we would not require any example . . . but that we are not".

The great advantage of Bhakti-Yoga is that it is the easiest and most natural way to realization, because it provides an embodiment of God which makes an appeal to the devotee in a personal way. But its drawback is the possibility of "theological imperialism", when the belief arises that one particular ideal is *the* ideal, and all others are false. Hence, Christians will often argue that their theology is totally unlike the theology of any other religion, because it alone is based, not on man's attempts to discover the truth, but on the specific revelation made by Jesus Christ. Such a belief can, at best, make for a patronising attitude towards other faiths; at worst, it burgeons into fanaticism which insists that there has been but one Incarnation, and all the rest are to be denounced. As Vivekananda trenchantly expressed it: "All the weak and undeveloped minds in every religion or country have only one way of loving their own ideal, i.e. by hating every other ideal." One is reminded of the mediaeval consolation that pagans, heretics and unbelievers of all kinds were infallibly destined to roast in hell, whilst the faithful could gloat over their discomfiture for all eternity.

The mark of a fanatic is that he is always more interested in *who* said something than *what* was said. One of the most refreshing discoveries about reading the New Testament alongside, say, the Upanishads, is to find that they contain an identical message. But fanatics never trespass outside their particular paddock and therefore perpetuate the illusion that they have access to a unique revelation. The worst offenders in this respect are people who cling to the petticoats of "sensitives" and mediums, and repeat lame platitudes as if they were spiritually charged epigrams.

Happily, fanaticism is only a feature of rudimentary Bhakti-Yoga, and I would not wish to lay undue emphasis on the negative aspect of this approach. We have only to remember the quality of love shown by St. Francis to see that true devotion rapidly lifts a worshipper into a realm where adoration of the ideal is the be-all and end-all, and the devotee has neither time nor inclination to make invidious comparison with other ideals. He is lost in his Lord.

To worship is constantly to remember the Beloved, and gradually the aspirant comes to the stage where he desires nothing but God, and all else loses its attraction for him. To renounce the world in this way is nothing like as hard or as brutal as renunciation undertaken for purely intellectual reasons. For the follower of Bhakti-Yoga, there is neither harshness nor dryness, and there is no call for desperate attempts to repress or suppress. All passions and emotions are redirected towards the chosen ideal, and of all forms of renunciation, Bhakti-Yoga is the least violent, because it allows a person to satisfy his heart's desire, so that all his earlier desires die off for want of nourishment. All the emphasis is on affirmation as the devotee cheerfully gives himself unreservedly to his Beloved and accepts whatever comes as a manifestation of love: by attaching himself so firmly to his personal God, he automatically breaks all other attachments.

For the Hindu, Ishwara, the God of Love, is neither separate nor different from Brahman, but rather the highest manifestation of the Absolute Reality, what Vivekananda called "the highest possible reading of the Absolute by the human mind". Such a Personal God is in fact the impersonal God seen through the mists of sense, and fulfils our need to crystallize our love round the Real Centre, the ultimate ideal.

Christ's reality to a Christian depends on the extent to which he has realized the Christ within, and has little to do with biblical scholarship or regular church attendance. No amount of quotation will make up for living out an ideal for oneself. "What Jesus, or Buddha, or Moses did is nothing to us, unless we too do it for ourselves", said Vivekananda: "You have to *become* the Bible, and not to follow it."

The Sanskrit word *ishta* means that way which is right for an individual, as he sees it, and every single person has his ishta which it is incumbent upon him to follow, if he is to be true to himself. Each person's vision of reality is peculiar to himself, and each therefore sees God according to his own nature. Once the devotee fastens onto an ideal, he is directing his attention to an aspect of God which makes a deep appeal to him. This is not like selecting an ideal in dilettante fashion at a kind of celestial supermarket; when it comes down to it, we have no option but to pick the conception of God which makes most sense to us. Once the ideal has been taken up, then there can be no chopping and changing, but there must be real perseverance until the goal of realization has been reached.

By concentrating on Jesus or Krishna, it does not follow that the spiritual giants of other ages and cultures should be regarded as in any way *infra dig*. In Vivekananda's view, to accept only *one* prophet as divine is to identify with a group, and this is politics and not religion. The Swami gave the bold advice that we should take all the old messages, support them with our own realizations, and then become a prophet to others. He himself asserted that he had found it possible in his life to worship all the prophets of the past, and to be ready for all that were yet to come.

None can deny the value of an image to focus devotion, and this image can be anything from an effigy to a mental picture: it furnishes the mind with something definite upon which to meditate. But while it is not wrong to say that the image is God, it is a grave mistake to think God is the image. A portrait may be a good likeness, but it can never be the subject itself, and idolatry begins with the failure to differentiate between the two.

For the bhakta, God appears in a variety of forms; it is a matter of one step at a time. At first, the relationship is often experienced as that of master and servant, or father and son—as so many prayers bear witness—a relationship in which the devotee seeks to carry out his Heavenly Father's instructions. Later may come the idea of God as a friend, and service ceases to be a duty and becomes more of a pleasure and a delight. Others find God most appealing in the form of a child, which accounts for the perennial popularity of the infant Jesus, and the Christmas story, where God appears as supremely vulnerable and subject to human frailty. Many mystics have spoken of the Great Lover, and nuns, of course, are described as "brides of Christ"—this conception of God enables the worshipper to enter into the most intimate contact with another which we know, that of sexual union. When God is thus embraced as the Beloved, the female soul is impregnated with the divine seed, and realization must surely follow. "As a father to his son, as a friend to his friend, as a lover to his beloved, be gracious unto me, O God" runs the *Gita*.

All these ideas of God are dualistic, in that they envisage a separation between Creator and created which can only be bridged by love. God is the Almighty Other, the Supreme King to Whom we owe our life and love. However He may be pictured—be it as Father, Friend, or Lover—He is divided from us, just as we are divided from each other. But this is the grand illusion, as will finally become evident to the bhakta who persists in his bhakti. By idealizing God, we make Him acceptable to us, but we rob both Him and ourselves of true identity, and there remains one final step for the pilgrim who would enter the Kingdom of Heaven. The formula TAT TVAM ASI—that you are—contains the answer to the riddle, and all the sages from the beginning of time have been trying in their different ways to elucidate those three words. The following Persian parable goes some way towards making TAT TVAM ASI meaningful:

"One came and knocked at the house of the Beloved. And a voice asked from within: Who is there? Then he who stood without the door replied: It is I. Then said the voice: This house will not hold Me and Thee; and the door was not opened. Then went the lover into the wilderness and fasted and prayed in solitude. And after many moons he returned again, and again he knocked at the door and again the voice asked: Who is there? and the lover replied: It is Thyself; and the door was opened unto him.''

Before we leave the subject of Bhakti-Yoga, it will be as well to mention the qualities required of those who aspire to love the Personal God. Above all else, what is needed is purity—purity at all levels. In the early stages, an aspirant should look to his diet and avoid eating "impure" foods, because it is vain to hope for spiritual insights until the physical body has become a fit vehicle to receive them. The bhakta must control his emotions, restrain his impulses and refuse to give way to the demands of the lower self. He should cultivate *ahimsa* or non-injury and the test of this is the extent to which he can genuinely rejoice in the success of an enemy, and not feel jealous or envious. Great physical and mental strength is needed, and a cheerful attitude should be cultivated. Desire for God must be all-consuming, the equivalent of a drowning man's desire for air.

Until purity has been attained, there is not the slightest chance of seeing God, so that energy should be used, not for running here there and everywhere in search of enlightenment, but in "polishing the mirror". Thus and only thus can the aspirant make himself ready for the coming of the Lord. With the attainment of purity, and not before, will come the awakening of love, and with that awakening will come that vision which is called beatific. "Blessed are the pure in heart, for they shall see God" is no idle promise—all who have achieved such purity will vouch for its truth. The *Gita* complements the Gospels with Krishna's assurance that "only by love can men see me, and know me, and come unto me".

Vivekananda's lectures in the West place far more emphasis on the Advaita proposition that All is One, than on the idea of devotion to a Personal God. At times, one almost gets the impression that, for Vivekananda, Bhakti-Yoga was a soft option compared with the other forms of yoga. Yet this is a false impression, because throughout his life, the Swami's heart never ceased to be moved by the various manifestations of God: Kali, Ramakrishna, Jesus, Buddha, Krishna, Mohammed—he paid tribute to them all. Vivekananda's supreme achievement was to emphasise the presence of God in all *men*, however benighted or ignorant they might appear to be.

If we really believe in reincarnation, then it will be obvious that we must have worshipped many gods in our time. Each form of the Absolute is valuable insofar as it expresses the life within, and each level of worship serves its purpose. There is a time for reverence, and a time for joy in God; there is a time for an insatiable desire for the Beloved, and a time for inconsolable grief at His absence. There is or will be a time when everything is seen as sacred because it belongs to God. But ultimately and inevitably, it will no longer be a question of a time for any *particular* experience of God, for our love will have grown so large that all differences will have gone, and there will be no "I" to worship any more. We shall then be able to say without blasphemy that "I and the Father are One"; but till that realization comes, we must hold fast to our chosen ideal, and persevere until we can see that this ideal is worshipped by all sects, under all names, and through all forms—for it is the One without a second. "The Self is the eternal subject, and we are struggling all the time to objectify that Self", declared Vivekananda. "The highest objectification of the Self possible to us is the Personal God . . . the highest imagination that can break all the links of the chain of bondage is that of the Personal God".

Bhakti-Yoga, therefore, attracts those who feel lonely and are "heavy-laden": the beauty of it is that, in the end, the pain of loneliness gives way to the joy of aloneness when the devotee becomes so absorbed in his worship, that he ceases to cherish his independent existence; and by loving his Lord, he is delivered from the bondage of separateness and realizes the eternal truth of I AM.

Chapter Sixteen

TAMING THE SLAYER
OF THE REAL

"I can't hear myself think." (Popular saying)

It is a chastening experience to sit down and do nothing, because in no time at all one becomes aware of the myriad voices which are all trying to make themselves heard in the babel of the mind. If most of us were to attempt a faithful transcription of our thoughts for a quarter of an hour, we should quickly realize that "stream-of-consciousness" writers are doing no more than approximating to the truth, and that conventional novelists edit life out of all recognition.

Vivekananda likened the mind to a maddened monkey, restless by nature, drunk with the wine of desire, stung by the scorpion of jealousy at the success of others and possessed by the demon of pride.

The restlessness of the mind becomes most obvious when we are either over-tired or suffering from a high temperature. However desperate the body's need for sleep, thoughts come and go with the appalling energy of angry hornets and, try as we may, it is impossible to follow any train of thought through to its conclusion. In fact, this lack of concentration is a chronic condition, and it will be found that to hold the mind to one thing for more than a few seconds is almost impossible. Our whole culture is based on the assumption that no one wishes to consider anything for long, and the media pander to this frailty by providing an incessant miscellany of unrelated bits and pieces to stuff into our already overloaded heads. The most cursory inventory of the mind's furniture will reveal a grotesque collection of images, ideas, and assorted "facts" which surface with the random whirl of a fruit machine as different experiences trigger things off.

Few would answer in the affirmative, if asked whether they were drunk with the wine of desire, because we are not given to oriental hyperbole. But in sober truth, we are beset by a howling horde of undisciplined cravings, which rarely give us a respite. "I want to be alone . . ." "I want to watch my favourite TV programme, but *she* insists on the other channel!" "I want a drink of tea/coffee/beer/whisky/rum . . ." "I want a cigarette . . ." "I want you . . .". etc., etc. So maybe the orientals aren't so hyperbolical after all.

We have already touched on one's feelings about other people's success in the previous chapter; it is extraordinarily difficult not to be jealous when all the plums seem to fall into the other fellow's lap and not ours. As for the demon of pride—well, pride is just another name for egotism, for the belief that I am more important than anyone else, more sensitive, significant, perceptive, brilliant, strong . . . in short, plain "special". The fact that other people don't seem to be as aware of this as they should be, is because they lack vision.

Raja-Yoga is the art of mind-control, and it must be confessed that this is no easy task. Vivekananda explained that what Raja-Yoga involves is turning the mind outside in and concentrating all one's powers on the goal of reaching self-knowledge; but what exactly did he mean by turning the mind outside in? In order to understand this idea, one has to examine the nature of perception.

Aldous Huxley in his classic study, *The Art of Seeing*, made it plain that sensing is not the same as perceiving; in other words, the eyes and the nervous system do the sensing, but it is the mind that does the perceiving. Clarity of vision, in every sense, hinges on accurate sensing and correct perception. Huxley produced the equation, SENSING + SELECTING + PERCEIVING = SEEING, and he went on to suggest that vision comes to those who have learnt to put their minds and eyes into "a state of alert passivity, of dynamic relaxation".

Vivekananda went rather further than Huxley in his analysis of perception. When we say that we "see" something, very complicated processes are at work. Obviously physical eyes are needed, but they in turn rely on the optic nerve in the brain. The mind receives the impression, but the *interpretation* of the incoming message rests with the Buddhi, that is the determinative faculty of the mind, sometimes translated as "intellect". Even that is not the end of the story: beyond the Buddhi lies the Atman, which denotes both the individual soul and Supreme Self. Hence Vivekananda's equation would be as follows:

$$\text{ATMAN} + \text{INTELLECT} + \text{MIND} + \text{BRAIN} + \text{EYES} = \text{PERCEPTION}$$

To turn the mind outside in, is therefore to prevent the mind from getting so caught up in the external world that there is no energy left over to explore the limitless possibilities of inner space. Our malady is that we have been turned inside out, and have consequently lost touch with God. Raja-Yoga is designed to regain contact with the divine essence, and release the potential which has lain dormant for so long. This is no task for the weak, and the aspirant must have unbounded faith and hope in himself; not of course in his ego, but in his true Self. Unless the mind is brought under control, then it will tear its owner up to pieces mercilessly. (It is not without significance that so many people in our culture suffer from mental illness because they have, in a very real sense, been ripped apart by their own undisciplined minds).

For those with a Christian upbringing, it is sometimes difficult to approve of the idea of affirming one's strength. The notion has become engrained that true humility consists of believing that we are "miserable sinners", people who "are not worthy to gather up the crumbs under Thy Table" and so on. The Prayer Book abounds in such sentiments, and, up to a point, these sentiments are true: a human being who is unaware of his own divinity *is* "a miserable sinner", but it is surely perverse to take such a partial view of man's nature. Certainly Vivekananda saw little to recommend this approach, and Raja-Yoga is based on the assumption that nothing is impossible for the man who has achieved mental control. "Through concentration of the mind, everything can be accomplished," promised the Swami, "even mountains can be crushed to atoms." Little progress can be expected in the aspirant who starts off with the crippling assumption that there is no health in him, and that he is fundamentally "unworthy".

According to Vedanta's teaching, the universe is composed of Akasha which can be seen only when it has taken form. Akasha is driven by the power of Prana, which is really force or energy, and this is the vital force in every living being. Vivekananda explained that to lay hold on Prana is to grasp the very secret of life, and he who controls Prana, controls everything. Pranayama, therefore, is far more than a system of breathing exercises. Certainly control of the physical breath will conduce to bodily health, but the Raja-Yogi seeks to gain mastery, not only of the breath, but of the nerve currents, thoughts, and finally of Prana itself.

The spinal column contains two nerve currents which are called Pingala and Ida, and a hollow canal runs through the spinal cord known as Sushumna. In the average person, the Sushumna is blocked, although occasionally a small amount of energy may rise from the Muladhara at the base of the spine. The aim of Pranayama is to unblock this canal, thus enabling the freed energies to rise up the Sushumna until they eventually reach the brain. This rousing of Kundalini, as it is called, can be terrifying, and those who have undergone the experience, speak of feeling as if their bodies were on fire, their minds shattered, and their very bones pulverized. Yet Kundalini must be awakened for superconscious perception to be attained.

Mention has already been made in an earlier chapter of the transmutation of sexual energies, and the practitioner of Raja-Yoga, just as much as the bhakta, must be pure if he is to be successful. Concentration can all too easily be harnessed to selfish ends, and the aspirant has always to be sure he is not allowing himself to be seduced by the Siddhis (powers) which come to him on the way.

For the necessary purity to be achieved, the mind has to be

totally emptied of the impressions of the past, and this is like stirring up the mud at the bottom of a lake. Beginners are often appalled at what comes to the surface, once they start in earnest on this process of dredging. Everything that was formerly subconscious must be made conscious, because until this has been done, all actions will be dictated by unconscious bias.

The most difficult stage of Raja-Yoga is that of Pratyahara which means "gathering towards" and consists of learning how to attach or detach the mind at will, refusing to be bullied or cajoled by pressures from outside. This, as has been suggested, is to turn outside in, to gather the mind from the thraldom of the senses. Raja-Yoga is learning how to bottle up the mind at will, and only letting the genie out, as and when required.

Once this stage has been reached, the aspirant can begin to develop his powers of concentration, and seek to apply all his energies to one thing at a time. Needless to say, this needs a good deal of practice, and the mind will kick like an unruly horse against the restraints imposed upon it.

The mind also hates to be disturbed, and new ideas seem abhorrent because they mean upheaval, just when everything appears to be nicely organized. Followers of Raja-Yoga must needs be thoughtful people, with a capacity for assimilating new ideas without being thrown off balance. Vivekananda contended that the more thoughtful a man is, "the more complicated will be the streets in his brain, and more easily he will take to new ideas and understand them". When the "streets" just aren't there, then they have to be constructed, and frequently, the work involved is felt to be too painful to be borne. It is hardly surprising that the Swami attached such importance to perseverance in the practice of Raja-Yoga, because the temptation must so often arise of giving the whole thing up as a bad job. "If you are brave enough, in six months you will be a perfect yogi," he claimed, and this emphasis on courage goes hand in hand with his insistence on the need for strength of purpose. It has been said that Vivekananda's whole life was in itself a concentration so profound, that, to anyone else, it would have been the most terrible asceticism, and his powers of unbroken concentration can be attributed to his constant devotion. Raja-Yoga, in other words, is far more than some kind of "mind dynamics": it is a discipline which would be impossible without the fuel of love and the goal of freedom. The aim is to rise above both the subconscious and the conscious levels of the mind and move into the superconscious; for this to be achieved, it is necessary to transcend reason, but never to deny it.

The subconscious is instinctual, and as far as it goes, almost infallible, but its range is very limited, and as soon as something new comes, it is baffled. The conscious is eminently reasonable, and has a larger scope than instinct, but it is by no means foolproof, and very slow besides. The superconscious, however, is absolutely reliable and far less circumscribed; but, of course, it is only available to those who have allowed it to develop. We don't become superconscious by chance.

Raja-Yoga is a means of speeding up the process of spiritual growth, and this necessarily involves rigorous training, in which any kind of vagueness or woolliness is out of the question. Dogged application and unflagging zeal are required before inspiration begins to percolate through. Once the aspirant has mastered the art of one-pointed concentration and has spent enough time watching the processes of his own mind with hawk-like attention, he is a candidate for Samadhi. In the initial stages of this superconscious state, he will retain a sense of "I" as distinct, though not separate from God; later will come Nirvikalpa Samadhi when the Impersonal is realized, all feeling of ego is wiped out, and there is a total transformation of being. The mind which had formerly buzzed so diligently from flower to flower in search of nectar, becomes quiet as soon as it reaches the heart of the lotus, and tastes reality.

Once all the stages of Raja-Yoga have been accomplished, searching is over and there is no more pain; full knowledge is attained, and duty ceases to be binding. All differences have fallen away and the aspirant realizes that Self which is the source of all selves. No longer need he look to books, creeds, churches or teachers: he has reached journey's end, and defeated the machinations of the Slayer of the real—the mind. This is not to say that he is now mindless, but rather that he has gained access to the Universal Mind and knows *from experience* that all is not what it seems. As the recipient of real inspiration, he knows that there is no clash between faith and reason, and that what once was hypothesis, has now become incontrovertible fact.

It is sometimes thought that going into Samadhi is like entering a magical chamber in which all perplexities are answered and all problems solved. People forget that Samadhi is not a lucky break, but the culmination of intensely hard work. Vivekananda used to say humorously that if a fool were to go into Samadhi, he would come out a sage; but, of course, fools don't go into Samadhi in the first place! What the Swami meant was that unimaginable clarity of vision is vouchsafed to those who experience the higher levels of consciousness, and all superstitions and fanaticisms fall away as illumination takes place. All that went before, now stands revealed as inchoate and embryonic; the soul had yet to be born. "When you step beyond thought and intellect and all reasoning," said Vivekananda, "then you have made the first step towards God; and that is the beginning of life." The proof of God lies in direct perception, in seeing Him "face to face", and this must infallibly yield transcendental knowledge—such is the reward of Raja-Yoga.

To recapitulate, he who would tread the path of the Raja-Yogi, must first learn to obey the rules of good conduct, secondly cultivate and establish purity, and thirdly, achieve a rock-like steadiness in all conditions. After that, he can practise breath-control, and seek to detach his mind from the countless external stimuli to which it is subjected. In the more advanced stages, he must learn how to fix his attention unwaveringly on whatever his will directs, and meditate to such effect that the gap between mind and object is closed, and he is able completely to identify with the object of meditation. Finally, he is ready to enter Samadhi which brings illumination, absorption and liberation. "Then," wrote Patanjali, "then, action and affliction come to an end . . . nothing remains to be achieved", and the power and the glory of the Self become manifest. Probably the most encouraging thing that Vivekananda ever said, was that every single person will eventually reach this point: no one will be left behind. As for the time it takes? That is entirely up to us. It is strange indeed that we can brook any delay, but when it comes to God, it is astonishing how many alternatives seem more attractive—for a while. "Not yet, Lord, not yet!" we cry, but God is nothing if not patient—He can wait forever and ever, and He always gets his man in the end.

Chapter Seventeen

THE LAST RESORT

"Our business is to wake up." (Aldous Huxley)

As has already been suggested, it is misleading (and indeed invidious) to distinguish too sharply between one kind of yoga and another. Vivekananda made it clear that realization can be attained "whether by work, or worship, or psychic control, or philosophy—by one, or more, or all of these". Although the theme for this chapter is to be that of Jnana-Yoga, my aim will be to draw the threads together at this point, in addition to considering the path peculiar to the jnani. The Swami said of himself that he was bhakta within and jnani without, whereas Ramakrishna was a jnani within and a bhakta without: in other words, for all his championship of the Advaita philosophy, Vivekananda had a devotional side to his nature which his audiences were frequently not aware of at all. Nevertheless *viveka* does mean the faculty of distinguishing between the real and the unreal, and Vivekananda lived up to his adopted name by making this the kernel of his message.

The jnani is one who follows the path of reasoning and discrimination to realize Ultimate Truth; to discriminate, that is, between the real and the unreal, and to renounce the unreal in favour of the real. This is not a suitable or congenial way for most people, because the mass of mankind are not constructive, analytical thinkers and have neither the inclination nor the capacity to ache over an idea until they have made it their own. They are content to leave others to do their thinking for them, and as far as religion goes, that means relying on the priests. History has shown that those who have had the temerity to break with hallowed tradition have always been branded as heretics (or "deviants" in more recent times), and their fate has tended to be more or less frightful, depending on the spirit of the age. Thinking has, in fact, always been a minority pursuit, and Socrates stands as the prototype of the man who insists on standing by the truth even when it means dying for it.

The true philosopher, the jnani, has one desire, and one desire only, to know the truth; and, to this end, he is prepared to make immense sacrifices. By the inexorable process of "Neti, neti", "Not this, not this", he will jettison one thing after another, as soon as he discovers that they serve no *ultimate* purpose. Diogenes ended up with no more than a barrel, while Tota Puri, who came to teach Ramakrishna, was nicknamed "Nangta" which means the Naked One: for him, even a barrel was an encumbrance.

"The jnani," said Vivekananda, "is a tremendous rationalist; he denies everything." In his passion for freedom, he is ready to suffer without a murmur of complaint, steadfastly faithful to the proposition that nothing is real apart from the One, the True Self, God. He is not prepared to take anything on trust; all must be hammered out on the anvil of personal experience, and tested until it is *seen* to be valid. He cannot afford to be frightened of anything, because there is no greater ally of ignorance than fear. Consequently he will make sure that all the experiences he dreads most, come his way, so that he can do battle with them. At the end of George Orwell's *1984*, Winston Smith is taken to the dreaded Room 101 where prisoners have to face whatever, for them, is the ultimate horror. A true jnani would not be *taken* to Room 101: he would go there of his own accord.

For the jnani, there can be neither soft options nor easy answers, because he is committed to using his reason to the point of excruciation. He cannot accept any kind of authority, be it a person or an organization: truly, he ploughs a lonely furrow. Vivekananda was sure God would pardon a man who used his reason and could not believe, as against a man who believes blindly, instead of using the faculties he has been given. "Until you have attained realization, there is no difference between you and atheists. The atheists are sincere, but the man

145

who says that he believes in religion and never attempts to realize it, is not sincere." The organized religions look to a holy book, a saviour, or an exclusive revelation of some kind as their authority, but the follower of Jnana-Yoga can find no lasting solace in the apt quotation, the beloved Master or the timely vision, for he is beyond the pale of established faiths and has nowhere to lay his head. Vivekananda averred that the organized religions do more harm than good, "because they stop the growth of each one's individual development", and he strongly advised no one to be foolish enough to put his "neck into the trap".

Any belief which can be destroyed by empirical reasoning must immediately be discarded, and all "mystical" teaching should be exposed to the full blaze of the most rigorous scientific enquiry before it can be accepted; real religion may go beyond reason, but reason remains the only guide to reach its threshold. If the conventionally devout are told ("on good authority") that God in His Infinite Wisdom thinks it best that certain problems should remain Holy Mysteries, then the absence of an explanation is accepted with a good grace. Not so the jnani, who will always show a Holmesian penchant for *solving* mysteries. Too often the pleas of "I can't understand it!" or "It's beyond me!" are the signs of a reluctance or refusal to find answers, because the suspicion lurks that the greater one's knowledge, the greater will be one's responsibility. Vivekananda promised that "if the whole responsibility is thrown upon our shoulders, we shall be at our highest and best, when we have nobody to grope towards, no devil to lay blame upon, no Personal God to carry our burdens . . ." This realization can only be reached by transcending the limitations of the senses, and also the power of reasoning, so that access is gained to facts which could never have been reached by reason alone. That most rational of men, the jnani, can only reach the knowledge of the Perfect by going beyond reason via reason, and thereby escaping the confines of the cobweb woven by the spider mind.

In one of his lectures, Vivekananda showed how reality is

presented to the thoughtful seeker in different guises as he makes his journey. At first he thinks dualistically and conceives of millions of jivas or individual souls all subject to the will of God. The jiva "is" and was not therefore created; after death, there is the possibility of eternal life for the jiva, an eternal life wholly devoted to loving God. However, while any karma remains to be worked out, the jiva must go through a series of incarnations on earth, until a balance has been reached, when release can take place.

The next step for the jnani, is from dualism to what Vivekananda called "qualified monism", in which God is thought of as interpenetrating the entire universe. He alone remains constant, but nature changes, and the soul changes: nature takes fresh forms, and the soul contracts and expands, depending on good or evil conduct. All these souls were pure originally, but they have become tarnished, and can only regain their pristine purity through the mercy of God and by doing good deeds.

The third step is really a gigantic leap, when the jnani sees that his earlier ideas were dreams, and there is no jiva at all, and that in reality he was never born and never died. It was all maya. "If the universe is the effect, and God the cause, it must be the reproduction of God." With realization, the universe is seen to be God, "and the very God who has so long been external appears to be internal, as our own Self". This is Advaita.

Hence, the three steps of Vedanta can be summarized as first, seeing each thing as separate from every other; secondly, seeing each thing as related to every other; thirdly, realising that there is only One thing which we mistakenly interpret as the many.

In his book, *The Religious Experience of Mankind*, Ninian Smart speaks of two levels of truth in Advaita Vedanta, the "higher" and the "ordinary". Final truth lies beyond ordinary religious belief and practice, and by rising above the worship of God "out there", we can come to a knowledge of the Absolute "in here". While the "higher" Brahman can be described as

Satchitananda—Being, Consciousness and Bliss, the "lower" Brahman is more determinate and is personal. As Professor Smart puts it, "As it were, the Absolute manifests itself in a personal way as Creator of the grand illusion. The personal Lord is thus the great illusionist, though bound up with his own illusion. He too in the last resort is part of the grand illusion."

We are back to the idea of "disappearances" when sex, sect, creed, colour, birth and all other differentiations vanish with the knowledge that all men are divine in essence, and that all separations and categories are made in ignorance of the true state of things. The tireless discriminator between the real and the unreal will begin to understand how misleading the dimensions of time and space are. He will also start querying the whole concept of cause and effect and discover that his work is not to make the soul free, but to get rid of all the bondages. The Absolute is beyond our understanding, neither unknowable nor known, and the notion of God on His Throne directing operations must eventually be abandoned as "the personality of God vanishes, and the impersonality comes".

The task of the jnani is to reconcile the actual with the ideal, to identify the present life with life eternal, and the perennial temptation is to give up and slip back into that state of dazed stupefaction which is so fatally attractive to human kind. Like people freezing to death, we yearn to be allowed to go to sleep, to drift into subjective make-believe and forsake the pursuit of objective facts. There can be nothing more practical than concerning oneself with facts, and that is why Jnana-Yoga is a supremely sensible discipline. A key fact, which has already been considered, is that we are infinitely strong although we have been foolish enough to believe we are weak. "Faith in ourselves will do anything . . . never tell yourselves or others that you are weak . . . what is there to be taught more in religion than the oneness of universe and faith in one's self?" This was Vivekananda's constant message, and he never ceased to stress the practicality of religion because it enables a man to be truly effective and to fulfil his destiny, instead of running aimlessly about chasing moonbeams. All notions of limitation must be thrown off, and gradually it will become evident to the pilgrim that the Celestial City which he seeks is not over the hills and far away, but lies within his own heart.

Vivekananda often referred to the value of being a witness to life instead of devoting all one's energies to augmenting a bogus sense of self-importance. As he saw it, we are not individuals yet, but are struggling towards individuality; significance begins for those whose life is in the whole universe, but "the more we concentrate our lives on limited things, the faster we go towards death". Progress, as generally understood, means altering the outer environment for the better and is associated with activities like slum clearance or the building of hospitals. Such measures can only be palliative, because real progress only comes with a fundamental change of attitude towards poverty and disease. What has to be understood is that by changing oneself, the whole world is changed, that by adjusting the microcosm, the macrocosm will automatically match whatever level of consciousness has been attained. Hence, "inner" work is always far more effective than "outer" work, in the long run, because the priorities are right. If a man wishes to chop wood he needs adequate lighting, good eyesight and a sharp axe. Advocates of "progress" seem too often to start work with a blunt axe, myopic vision and poor light.

It is sometimes thought that the Advaita philosophy is so "inhuman" and stark, that it will rob a man of all initiative. Somehow to work for the "collective" is much less congenial than working for oneself. This is to confuse totalitarianism with oneness: the Advaitist sees that it is not a question of "me" serving "them", but of "I" being "That". There is neither contraction nor expansion, but simply a recognition of the truth, "that which is self-luminous cannot decay".

If only we can shake off our ignorance, then we can become what we really are, and it will be seen that we have been deluded as to our true identity. What Vivekananda called "the real perceiver, the real enjoyer, the being in the body" is the

149

Atman who is working the body by means of the mind. The Atman alone is immaterial, and the Atman alone is real being identical with the Self: as in the individual, so in the universal.

The jnani finally realizes that he is neither body nor mind, but has reached the goal and can proclaim triumphantly, "I am He!" "This", said the Swami, "this is true knowledge, and all reason and intellect, and everything else, is ignorance."

"Where is knowledge for me, for I am knowledge itself! Where is life for me, for I am life itself! I am sure I live, for I am life, the one Being, and nothing exists except through me, and in me, and as me. I am manifested through the elements, but I am the free One. Who seeks freedom? Nobody. If you think that you are bound, you remain bound; you make your own bondage. If you know that you are free, you are free this moment. This is knowledge, knowledge of freedom. Freedom is the goal of all Nature."

Chapter Eighteen

SPOKES IN THE WHEEL

'Irrevocable commitment to any religion is not only intellectual suicide: it is positive unfaith because it closes the mind to any new vision of the world. Faith is, above all, openness—an act of trust in the unknown." (Alan Watts)

Humanists, like Bertrand Russell, have often pointed to the fact that there has been no greater divider of mankind than that of religion. The iniquities and enormities of the Inquisition apart, the history of Christianity has been an appalling story of persecution, massacre, and spiritual rape. Again and again, Western Europeans have gone on the warpath, sword in one hand and Bible in the other, and although no one can dispute the excellence of some missionary activity, much of it has been deeply resented by people whose code of ethics was often far ahead of those who sought to "convert" them.

This is not the place to make a catalogue of atrocities: suffice it to say that many followers of certain religions (particularly Christianity and Islam) have, at different times, succumbed to the worst excesses of fanaticism. The most horrible thing about fanatics is that they feel entitled (indeed morally bound) to torture, maim and destroy anyone who does not agree with them, and the fact that they are frequently sincere is small consolation to anyone who has had the misfortune to fall into their hands.

The "true believer's" bloodcurdling zeal stems from the notion that he and his kind have lighted upon the "truth", and anyone who fails to share this version of truth must be either wilful, obtuse or invincibly ignorant. Nothing disturbs such people more than any kind of untidiness, and this explains their enthusiasm for uniformity and hatred of the misfit. To the Nazi mind, for example, Jews, homosexuals, intellectuals, mental defectives and the like, were a blot on the Nordic escutcheon, so the Final Solution was therefore to "liquidate" them, thereby purging the Master Race of its toxic elements.

Fanatics, in their craving to "belong", develop the capacity to defend their chosen truth with astonishing tenacity and the utmost ingenuity, because they have so totally identified with the cause they have espoused. Were they to defect, not only would they be ostracized by their former associates, but worse, they would have undermined their own inner foundations and left themselves nothing to stand on. So great is the fear of this calamity, that "true believers" protect themselves by blocking off any disturbing evidence or challenging ideas, and have a mortal aversion to people who ask questions. The intellectually nimble fanatic learns how to cope with questions, by becoming an expert in his particular field, and acquiring the flexibility and bounce of the skilled casuist which allows for urbanity and good humour, as criticisms are brushed off like troublesome flies.

Vivekananda said that he feared the old superstitions would take a long time to run out; the supporters of each rival belief would do all they could to perpetuate their own creeds and loyalties. The ideas of the family brother, the caste brother, the national brother were not likely to die out overnight, and certainly the history of the last 80 years indicates a sorry failure to act on the idea of the brotherhood of man. The twentieth century could, with justice, be called the age of fanaticism.

However, side by side with all the antagonisms and conflicts, there has also grown up an attitude of acceptance and tolerance which is increasingly widespread, and gives us some reason to be optimistic. A few years ago, the Second Vatican Ecumenical Council issued a *Declaration on the Relation of the Church to Non-Christian Religions* in which the emphasis was on what men have in common and what draws them into fellowship together. The *Declaration* concedes that "from ancient times down to the present day there is found in various peoples a certain recognition of that hidden power which is present in history and human affairs, and in fact sometimes an acknowledgement of a supreme Godhead, or even of a Father". The Vedantist may smile at the last phrase, but the fact remains that this is a Church of a different colour from the one which burnt heretics. "The Catholic Church rejects nothing which is true and holy in these (other) religions . . . she therefore urges her sons, using prudence and charity, to join members of other religions in discussions and collaboration." Nevertheless, when it comes to the crunch, Rome "proclaims, and is bound to proclaim unceasingly, Christ, who is 'the way, the truth, and the life'," and, according to Catholic orthodoxy, the Revelation of Jesus Christ is unique and Christians have access to ultimate truth in a way which is denied to all other religions. The very fact that the Catholic Church "rejects nothing which is true and holy" in other faiths, implies that there are elements in them which are neither true nor holy, so the wisest policy is to look to an authority which is *guaranteed* to be reliable. To differ from such an authority must infallibly be arrogance or ignorance and it can never be a question of selecting a religion to suit oneself; no, the religion is there to alter and trim the individual to fit it. All ways to spiritual growth may in a sense be valid, but they are not equal, and Christianity says that the supreme reality has stepped down to the beggar maid, and this has only happened once.

All such argument is based on Aristotelian logic which insists that a thing must either be true or false. So-called paradoxical logic, however, conceives of a thing being both true and false at the same time. It is important to appreciate how deeply conditioned the Western mind is in this matter of opting for a truth which apparently rules out other truths. Orientals approach problems in quite a different way, and will say something like this,

"All right, so that is how you see it, and you are perfectly right to accept that view as true. I see it in another way, but I do not deny your experience of reality. Until we attain to full realization, we can only speak in relative terms, and by sharing

153

each other's insights, we shall extend our knowledge and deepen our own appreciation of the Real. Let us talk together."

When Vivekananda attended Mass in America with Constance Towne, he was not doing this simply to please her: as the bell rang at the consecration and all heads were bowed in adoration of the presence of Christ on the altar, his hand touched hers, and he whispered, "It is the same God and Lord we both worship." The harmony of religions which he envisaged meant neither taking the best of each, nor stressing similarities and ignoring differences; for him, with all their differences, religions should live together harmoniously, and the only universal religion possible in his view, was the amity of religions. "Religion," he said, "is the acceptance of all existing creeds, seeing in them the same striving towards the same destination. Creed is something antagonistic and combative." He told the Parliament of Religions at its Final Session that each religion should assimilate the spirit of the others, without losing its own unique character in the process; and it was ridiculous to think of the exclusive survival of one religion at the expense of all the rest. "That which exists is One: sages call It by various names", so that although religions may differ in non-essentials, in essentials they are in agreement.

Vivekananda contended that all religions hail originally from Asia, and their survival or decline has depended entirely on whether they have or have not appealed to people as true. At different periods, different religions have been in the ascendant, and sects have been multiplying at an ever-increasing speed, especially in the last two hundred years. Provided they can tolerate each other, sects need not be condemned. When, for instance, Voltaire visited England, he remarked, "If there were only one religion in England, there would be danger of tyranny; if there were two, they would cut each other's throats; but there are thirty, and they live happily together in peace." Vivekananda's watchword was, "Every man his own sect" and his advice was to take any path you like, follow any prophet you like, but "to have only that method which suits your own nature". It is quite unrealistic to imagine that all will conform to the same ideas, and indeed, it would be utterly sterile if they did. The conflict between them can be creative and lead to growth until such time as the antagonists begin to realize that they do not differ as much as they at first thought. In the end, it begins to look as if seemingly contradictory opinions are both true at the same time. How can this be? Because each religion highlights one aspect of the great universal truth, "and spends its force in embodying and typifying that part of the great truth". Religions are not in conflict at all, but can be seen as both supplementary and complementary to each other. Even the most extreme and bizarre sect has got hold of a fragment of the truth, and if it were possible to accept *all* the fragments of *all* the sects, the resultant jigsaw would begin to make up an intelligible picture.

We can only take in as much truth as we are ready to receive, and each person is at a different stage of development. As the Swami remarked, "Give a man a whole museum of truths, he will at once take what is suited to him." It is no good trying to foist a truth upon him which, according to *his* lights, is seen either as false or irrelevant. A son may take a broader view than his father, but this does not mean that the father's conception of reality was wrong-headed. Equally, for some, a universal religion already exists because they are prepared for it; for others, the edicts and doctrines of one particular sect remain exclusively true. As the field of vision widens, the scope of truth increases in proportion, until in the end, it is impossible to keep Reality within the confines of any specific creed, because it becomes evident that All is One.

Each religion has its peculiar merit, and universality of approach grows from an appreciation of these different qualities. The strength of Islam lies in its emphasis on equality: all Moslems look on each other as equal in the eyes of Allah, irrespective of race, class or nationality. Hinduism stresses the supreme importance of renunciation, while Christianity admonishes us to purify our minds and hearts, and to be ready.

A universal religion must rest on *acceptance* rather than mere toleration, and ideally it should be all things to all men: philosophy to the philosopher, devotion to the worshipper, symbolism to the ritualist, and beauty to the poet. "We take in all that has been in the past, enjoy the light of the present, and open every window of the heart for all that will come in the future."

Vivekananda explained that a religion consists of three main ingredients: philosophy, mythology and ritual. All the clashes between religions are caused by these, and the heart of the matter gets overlooked in all the sound and fury of argument. If only it could be seen that unity in variety is the plan of the universe, then these differences would cease to be a source of conflict. "Through high philosophy or low, through the most exalted mythology or the grossest, through the most refined ritualism or arrant fetishism, every sect, every soul, every nation, every religion, consciously or unconsciously, is struggling upward, toward God . . ."

Hence the Swami's "little plan", as he called it, was neither to destroy nor to criticise any sincere belief, but to take a man where he stood, and from there give him a lift. Such an approach means recognising the infinite variety of human kind, and knowing that one man's creed is another man's prison. Active people, fitted for hard work and efficient organisation, will tend to be attracted to Karma-Yoga, whereas more aesthetic and devotional types are more likely to be drawn to Bhakti-Yoga. Others, with a taste for self-analysis are better suited to Raja-Yoga, and the philosophically inclined can tackle Jnana-Yoga. The perfectly balanced man would have all facets of his nature equally developed, and this would prevent his being lop-sided and prejudiced against those of a different temperament. Vivekananda once said that he would like to get extreme exponents of all the different types, shut them up in a room, and photograph their beautiful derisive smiles!

In his famous book, *The Varieties of Temperament—A Psychology of Constitutional Differences*, William Sheldon suggested that people can be divided into three broad divisions: viscerotonic-endomorphs, somatotonic-mesomorphs and cerebrotonic-ectomorphs.

The viscerotonic-endomorph is the "fat and jolly" kind of person, who is relaxed in posture and movement, and regards comfort and luxury as primary goals. He loves a good meal, epecially in company with others, and cannot have enough of polite ceremonies. He is not cursed with "the awful gift of discernment", and likes to be liked to the point of outright greediness for affection and approval. Isolation is anathema to him and he is fond of people simply because they *are* people! Slow to arouse emotionally, he places a high value on peace and quiet, sleeps like a log, and relaxes into good fellowship at the tilt of a glass. Such a person always shares his problems, never hides his feelings and likes the idea of being a child to such an extent that he in fact craves to return to infancy. This craving is matched by a strong aversion to death so that viscerotonics are not the kind to fall like ripe plums into the grave.

Because people like this are naturally gregarious, they take to the idea of brotherly love like ducks to water. In religion, they are strongly congregational in their practice, and delight in singing hymns and saying prayers together addressed to a Heavenly Father. They are also orientated towards a cult of divine childhood, and derive great pleasure from long and complicated rituals. Births, marriages and deaths are celebrated with much sacrament and ceremony, and all this creates for them the feeling that God is in his Heaven, and all's right with the world. Even the tragedy of death can be mitigated by a really decent funeral.

The world of the somatotonic-mesomorph is poles apart from all this: it is a world of instant action, vigorous movement and tough activities. The kind of hero depicted in war comics exactly embodies the type: bursting with energy, "born to command", always getting into scrapes, ruthless in the pursuit of his aims. Such a person is characterised by an unequivocal "stare", a bold directness of manner, and a complete freedom from squeamishness. He lacks self-awareness, because he is so caught up in "outer Reality", and this cuts him off from his own depths. Consequently he is easily converted to a new idea, because for him the novelty comes with the force of a revelation—he has never thought of it consciously before. A key characteristic of such people, who may be said "to think with their muscles", is that they are desperate to enjoy life before it is too late, are painfully alive to the passing of youth, and dread old age. Death, as such, holds no terrors for them: it is at least decisive.

In religion, somatotonics are all in favour of converting others to their faith, are quick to court martyrdom and display stoical and puritannical attitudes. God, for them is a gruff Commanding Officer—stern but just, and they serve Him dutifully by doing active good works. Tender conscience is, in their estimation, a form of self-indulgence, and loyalty to a cause far more admirable than a lonely adherence to a personal belief. If we want to clothe such a type in flesh and blood, we should think of Biggles of the RAF or Sapper's Bulldog Drummond—chaps who get things done with no shilly-shallying, and know what they want.

Finally we come to the "weeds" and the "swots"—the cerebrotonic-ectomorphs, those mournful skeletons at the feast of life. Like horses under tight rein, they carry their bodies stiffly with their hands clenched, their eyes bright and alert. Suffering as they do from extreme sensitivity in every respect, they tend to be mentally over-intense, emotionally apprehensive and physically insecure. The cerebrotonic hates above all else to be obvious, and takes infinite pains to conceal what he is feeling, even when his feelings are overwhelming. Anything but the life and soul of the party, he cringes in the face of the convivial, the hearty or the loud. Equipped with a tremendous range of mental and emotional response, the cerebrotonic's strained and tense facial expression gives nothing away to the observer. He is not good at enduring pain, sleeps badly and reacts unfavourably to alcohol. When troubled or perplexed, his instinctive desire is to get away and sweat out his problems on his own. Sheldon explains that "reality for him is essentially and foremost what he dredges up out of his own mental cellars. The outward reality appears to be secondary". He usually has an excellent insight into his own motives and is not easily converted. "The cerebrotonic" writes Sheldon, "suggests a form of life which has wandered a long way from its biological moorings, and has forgotten the way back." Such a person's lifelong quest is for "understanding" and for him, later life is the golden age, with childhood and youth seen as periods of preparation. Death is anticipated with delight and cerebrotonics like nothing better than a discussion about mortality and transience.

Of such is the kingdom of the mystics and contemplatives, the "outsiders" and the thinkers who are often ahead of their contemporaries, because they are less bound by convention. They are unmoved by ritual and cannot fathom how others can be bothered with it; yet it is probably true to say that the cerebrotonic has more sympathy with those of differing temperament, than vice versa, because he is more given to self-examination.

Sheldon's analysis should not be taken to mean that there are three distinct kinds of people: obviously most of us are of mixed type. But, for the present purpose, all I wish to indicate is how enormously temperaments differ. When it comes to religion, men's views about God are legion, despite the fact that they are all looking to the One True God. Vivekananda believed that if only each man could choose his ideal and stick to it, all religious controversy would vanish: trouble comes when people try to impose their ideal onto others. "If you have the power to worship God as spirit, good!" pronounced the Swami, "but there was a time when you could not." The very fact that the Advaita philosophy is the *last* word in religion and thought, means that there must be many preceding words leading up to it. Vivekananda thought that Advaita was the only position from which one can look upon all religions and sects with love, and he also saw it as the religion of future enlightened humanity. Certainly its great merits are that it is built upon principles rather than historical characters, that it is entirely in harmony with the discoveries of modern science, that it speaks of the universality of religions, and by accepting that All is One, is entirely free of bigotry or attitudes of rejection. An Advaitist cannot possibly be spiritually schizophrenic.

At the same time, it is no good imagining that the mass of the people are going to grasp this overnight. It takes an unconscionably long time for ideas to percolate through from top to bottom, and we have only to look about us to realise that few concern themselves with spiritual goals of any description. Yet, for all that, much is happening which is encouraging: recently, for example, the *News of the World* has been carrying a number of reincarnation stories. The approach may be sensationalistic, but such stories are now at least gaining currency. Again, there are a number of "New Age" centres where an attempt is being made to actualize ancient truths: there can be no doubt that the formerly esoteric is becoming ever more exoteric. This was a change which Vivekananda envisaged, and he was therefore a pioneer of the New Age; his slogans of "Help and not fight", "Assimilation and not destruction", "Harmony and peace and not dissension" are more relevant than ever for a world which could so easily collapse into chaos and old night.

Vivekananda knew full well that he was ahead of his time and that, in a sense, his message was premature. Since his death in 1902, there has been an unprecedented orgy of fighting, destruction and dissension. Maybe it has had to be as bad as this for humanity to wake up to the danger. The alarm bells are ringing now with a vengeance as experts in every field, from ecology to nuclear physics, tell us that Armageddon is on our doorstep. Salvation, according to Vivekananda, lies not in trying to make the world a better place, but in seeking to realize our own strength and inherent spirituality. Given such a realization, then the work will follow: without it, nothing of ultimate value can be accomplished. People are afraid that when they attain to realization, when they see that there is but One, "the foundations of love will be dried up, and everything in life will go away, and that all they love will vanish for them, in this life and in the life to come. People never stop to think that those who bestowed the least thought on their own individualities have been the greatest workers in the world . . . such a man becomes a world-mover for whom his little self is dead and God stands in his place." This is Vivekananda's message and unless we can put it into practice immediately, there will be no world to move. The choice is ours.

As I bring this little book to a close, I cannot but be conscious of its limitations. This is no book for the expert or the specialist: it is for the common reader. Possibly other books mentioned in the bibliography will appeal, but it is my hope that the gist at least of Swami Vivekananda's teachings are to be found in these pages. "Arise! Awake! and stop not until the goal is reached" he said in almost every lecture that he gave, and that is really all that remains to be said at this stage. The most that I dare add is simply this: Bon Voyage!

THE END

BIBLIOGRAPHY

THE MAN

Swami Vivekananda in America—New Discoveries, Marie Louise Burke. Advaita Ashrama.

The Life of Swami Vivekananda by his Eastern and Western Disciples (2 vols.). Advaita Ashrama.

Reminiscences of Swami Vivekananda by his Eastern and Western Admirers. Advaita Ashrama.

Ramakrishna and His Disciples, Christopher Isherwood. Vedanta Press, Hollywood.

The Master as I Saw Him, Sister Nivedita (Margaret Noble). Ubdodhan.

The Life of Vivekananda and the Universal Gospel, Romain Rolland. Advaita Ashrama.

THE MESSAGE

The Complete Works of the Swami Vivekananda in 8 volumes. Advaita Ashrama.

Swami Vivekananda in East and West, Editorial Advisers: Swami Ghanananda and Dr. Geoffrey Parrinder. Ramakrishna Vedanta Centre.

Swami Vivekananda Centenary Memorial Volume. Published by Swami Sambuddhananda.

GENERAL

Aphorisms of Yoga by Bhagwan Shree Patanjali done into English from the original in Samskrit with a commentary by Shree Purohit Swami and an introduction by W. B. Yeats. Faber.

The Bhagavad-Gita. Translated from the Sanskrit with an introduction by Juan Mascaró. Penguin.

Bibliography

The Dhammapada: The Path of Perfection. Translated from the Pali with an introduction by Juan Mascaró. Penguin.

The Flame and the Light—Meanings in Vedanta and Buddhism. Hugh I'Anson Fausset. Abelard-Schumann, London-N.-Y.

Vedanta for the Western World. Edited and introduced by Christopher Isherwood. Paperback, Unwin.

Krishnamurti—the Years of Awakening, Mary Lutyens. John Murray.

Hinduism, K. M. Sen. Penguin.

The Varieties of Temperament—A Psychology of Constitutional Differences, William Sheldon with S. S. Stevens. Copyright, Harper and Row, 1942. Hafner Publishing Co. N-Y and London, 1970, reprinted with minor corrections.

The Religious Experience of Mankind, Ninian Smart. Fontana.

The Oxford History of India. Vincent A. Smith, C.I.E. (3rd Edn). Edited by Percival Spear. Oxford University Press.

The Ten Principal Upanishads. Put into English by Shree Purohit Swami and W. B. Yeats. Faber.

The Upanishads, translations from the Sanskrit with an introduction by Juan Mascaró. Penguin.